Date Due

HOW FAMILY MEMBERS PERCEIVE EACH OTHER

Political and Social Attitudes in Two Generations

Richard G. Niemi

New Haven and London, Yale University Press, 1974

Library of Congress catalog card number: 73–86913
International standard book number: 0–300–01698–0

Designed by Sally Sullivan
and set in Times Roman type.
Printed in the United States of America by
The Colonial Press Inc., Clinton, Massachusetts.

Published in Great Britain, Europe, and Africa by
Yale University Press, Ltd., London.
Distributed in Latin America by Kaiman & Polon,
Inc., New York City; in Australasia and Southeast
Asia by John Wiley & Sons Australasia Pty. Ltd.,
Sydney; in India by UBS Publishers' Distributors Pvt.,
Ltd., Delhi; in Japan by John Weatherhill, Inc., Tokyo.

To Shirley

Contents

List of Tables and Figures

Tables

Figures

Preface

A recent article about the family appeared under the title "Family Sociology or Wives' Family Sociology?" (Safilios-Rothschild, 1969). Its point was that sociologists often rely on one respondent, usually the wife, for reports of the attitudes and behavior of the entire family. Sociologists are not the only ones who utilize this practice, of course, since many studies by psychologists, political scientists, and others also rely on a single family respondent.

This book is a study of some aspects of that practice. Are the data we get from one family member similar to what we get from other members of the same family? If not, what are the differences? Are reports consciously or unconsciously biased? In what direction? Or are misperceptions random insofar as we can tell? Are some kinds of families especially prone to erroneous and biased reports? Using a national sample in which two or three family members were independently interviewed, we are able to provide answers to these and other questions.

We also consider the methodological and substantive implications of some of our results. Do the misperceptions and biases make the family look more or less important in the transmission of values between generations? What can we learn from parents' perceptions of children about the processes of learning within the family? Do the reports from a single respondent make the family appear more homogeneous than it actually is?

A glance at the table of contents indicates that the material covers topics of interest to psychologists, sociologists, political scientists, and anyone studying the family. With regard to my own discipline, political science, I hope that the book also conveys my conviction that adequate measurement is at least as great a stumbling block in the development of a political science as, for example, the need for formal theory. More empirical work on measurement needs to be done, more innovative measuring techniques need to be developed, more analytic studies of the effects of measurement error are required; in general we require a much greater appreciation of the need for and the difficulty of arriving at adequate measurement techniques. Only recently have political scientists begun to realize the importance of this problem. Now that it is recognized, let us hope that more rapid progress will be made in solving it.

Since this book is derived from a large-scale investigation of political socialization, my debts are many. Foremost thanks go to Kent Jennings of the University of Michigan, with whom I have now been happily associated for close to ten years. He has read and commented on much of the manuscript; more generally, he has been a productive and competent coauthor and critic. I also wish to thank Roman Hedges, who was my research assistant in the later stages of analysis and who has also commented extensively on the manuscript. Similarly, thanks go to others who have read all or portions of the book—Ronald Inglehart, Kenneth Langton, Byron Massialas, Warren Miller, and Howard Schuman.

The study could not have been conducted without the assistance of the sampling and field staffs and numerous interviewers, coders, keypunchers, and research assistants at the Survey Research Center of the University of Michigan. To all of them I owe a debt of gratitude. The secretaries at the University of Rochester, Peg Gross and Janice Brown, deserve a special word of thanks.

Financial support for the original study was generously provided by the Danforth Foundation. Support for the analysis was provided by the National Science Foundation. In addition, the Computing Centers of the University of Michigan and the University of Rochester both provided computer time, ultimately supported by the National Science Foundation.

Chapter 3 was previously published in Dennis (1973), although tables 3.4 and 3.7 were left out of that version, and a cautionary note about aggregate reports has been added to the conclusion. A portion of chapter 4 will also be published in Jennings and Niemi (1974). Otherwise, the analysis is published here for the first time.

R.G.N.

Rochester, New York
May 1973

1: Introduction

Measurement is a critical element in the development of any scientific discipline. To the extent that adequate measurement is impossible or undeveloped, theoretical efforts and empirical work alike suffer. Lacking measures of key phenomena, theories are often untestable and/or take on the appearance of tautologies. Empirical work suffers more directly, for even straightforward descriptive work becomes more difficult the poorer our measurements are.

In the social sciences generally, and in political science specifically, vast improvements in existing measures are needed along with the development of innovative kinds of measures. The considerable effort that has been spent in the past several decades on the development of new and improved analysis methods, as well as the strides that have recently been taken toward the development of rigorous political theory, must now be matched by comparable gains in our measurement capabilities.

The present work represents a small step in that direction. It is an attempt to assess the accuracy of and to suggest improvements in one type of data—survey data about the family. The usual method of collecting information about the family raises severe problems. Information is most often obtained from the respondents who form the basic unit of analysis, without any attempt to verify independently their reports. Respondents are called upon to report the values, feelings, characteristics, and behavior of spouses, parents, and children and to assess the interaction between themselves and other family members. The ability of individuals to provide this type of information has been questioned repeatedly, and potential sources of error and bias have been identified and discussed.[1]

---

1. Support for this statement will be given below, since the kinds of errors and biases that are expected vary with the type of data under consideration. Briefly, however, response validity is questioned on one of three

While legitimate doubts have thus been raised about the reliability and validity of much family-level data, few studies have sought to confirm or deny their accuracy.[2] This book is such an attempt. An extensive investigation is undertaken of the reports of high school seniors and their parents. A wide array of topics is covered, including parents' and spouses' demographic characteristics, their political attitudes and behavior, the students' partisan commitment, as well as family structure and interaction among family members. A basic feature of the analysis will be to match students with their parents and husbands with their wives in order to compare responses to identical questions, thus ascertaining the amount of student-parent and husband-wife agreement. When little agreement is found, an effort will be made to explain the observed discrepancies and to suggest ways of improving future data collection.

My focus is primarily methodological, and the coverage is of sufficiently broad scope that it should be of interest to anyone collecting data about the family. But since my inquiry is derived from a larger study of political socialization, some of the substantive consequences for this field of study will also be discussed. The origins of the study also explain the emphasis on political data (chaps. 3, 4, and 6).

---

grounds (or some combination thereof): a) the family is a sensitive topic so that reports are constrained by social acceptability; b) the desired information is about persons other than the respondent himself so that lack of knowledge as well as perceptual distortion may be important factors; and c) questions about the family are often of the recall variety.

2. Neither the term "reliability" nor "validity," as conventionally used, expresses precisely the kind of tests undertaken here. Nor would the looser term "accuracy" always be appropriate. For example, the comparisons of student and parent and of husband and wife reports of family structure (chaps. 5 and 8) bear a strong resemblance to testing for interrater reliability, but the "raters" in this case are obviously not dealing with exactly the same material. Similarly, a number of my comparisons could be said to measure concurrent validity or simply accuracy. However, this implies the presence of a standard against which to compare a set of data. Here we cannot be sure that the "standard" itself is always correct. My solution is a) to use the terms "reliability" and "validity" together or interchangeably (where appropriate the term "accuracy" will also be used) and b) to make explicit in each chapter exactly what I am assuming about the comparisons being made in that chapter. On reliability and validity in general, see Kerlinger (1964, chaps. 24–25) and Selltiz et al. (1959, chap. 5).

No study of this kind can claim to be definitive. It is always possible that other types of questions, other kinds of samples, different time periods, and so on, would yield results different from those presented here. But this study is based on the kind of sample and contains the wide array of data that permits far greater and more generalizable analyses than have been done previously for the subject areas covered. Thus, while I cannot hope to answer every question that analysts have in mind, I will provide a much firmer basis for judging the reliability and validity of data that have been collected and for improving data collection in the future. Happily, the data on which this study is based are available from the Inter-University Consortium for Political Research (University of Michigan). Additional analysis is thereby made possible if there are gaps that readers wish to fill.

COLLECTION OF FAMILY-LEVEL DATA

To question the validity of family-level data as usually collected does not imply that better methods are necessarily available. It is true that a variety of methods have been used. Observation and experimental techniques were used by March (1953–54), Strodtbeck (1951), and Kenkel (1963) to study husbands' and wives' decision-making processes and in a large number of studies of parent-child interaction (Lytton, 1971). Census data were used by Greenstein (1965) and Tolley (1973) to assign the families of their sample children to a social class, while Hess and Torney (1967, pp. 228–29) sometimes turned to school records. Hollingshead (1949) used local citizens as raters and Sewell and Haller (1956) used teachers as raters for the same purpose. For elite populations, public records have been used by Matthews (1954, 1960), Dogan (1961), Guttsman (1961), Frey (1965), Ranney (1965), Valen (1966), and others. All of these methods are useful for some types of analysis, but they are obviously not suitable for most general purposes. The information available in public records is highly restricted, being limited to certain populations and to certain types of factual information. Observations and experimentation require a degree of cooperation not usually given to researchers. In addition, time and cost factors prohibit large-scale use of these techniques.

An alternative method is to gather data from more than one family member. Interviews with the parents of sample children have frequently been conducted, although usually with small, specialized samples (Hyman, 1959, pp. 70–71; Maxwell et al., 1961; Hoffman and Lippitt, 1960, pp. 976–79; Kohn and Carroll, 1960; Helpter, 1958; Hess and Goldblath, 1957; Radke, 1946).[3] This is not a satisfactory alternative, however, since parents are often less accessible (as when questionnaires are distributed in schools) or no longer living (as for adult samples). The procedure is costly in any event. Even if parents can be questioned, additional problems are raised. While information about a parent may be more accurate if it comes from him or her rather than from a child, there are questions about the family for which parents' reports may be no more accurate than children's. And unless both parents are questioned, we must still rely on the child's or spouse's report about the other parent. Interviewing both husband and wife is perhaps a more feasible task than interviewing children and parents, though some of the same difficulties are encountered. In any event, interviewing both parents seems inefficient if only one or two items about the spouse are needed.

The difficulties associated with other methods of gathering family-level data have resulted in the vast majority of political socialization studies (and studies of the family in general) relying exclusively on respondents' reports about the family—chiefly reports about parents. The respondents from whom this information was sought have varied from young children to adult populations, and the instruments have been both interviews and written questionnaires. The study reported in Hess and Torney (1967) and Easton and Dennis (1969) was based on second through eighth grade respondents, while Greenstein (1965) relied on data from fourth through eighth grade students and Andrain (1971) on fifth and eighth graders. Remmers (1959, 1963) and others have used responses of high school students extensively. College students have

3. In a few cases interviews have been held with more than one child in the family or with entire families. See, for example, Schramm et al. (1961, p. 199).

been used as respondents at least since Allport's study in 1928 (Hyman, 1959, p. 79).

Reports by adults of their childhood experiences are widely used. Examples include the voting studies by Berelson et al. (1954) and by Campbell et al. (1960), as well as studies of political elites such as legislators and party activists. Respondents in well over a dozen countries have been asked about their family environment. Pinner (1965) asked Dutch, Belgian, and French university students about their family backgrounds, while Langton (1969) inquired about the background of Jamaican secondary school students. Almond and Verba (1963) asked English, Italian, German, Mexican, as well as American adults to recall their family experiences, while Butler and Stokes (1969) concentrated on British respondents. Willis (1956) questioned Swedish adults, and Valen and Katz (1964) asked leaders of Norwegian political parties about the political interest and party identification of their parents. In the adult studies, questions have usually been included about spouses as well.

The information gathered has varied as widely as the samples from which it was collected. Many studies have relied on children's and spouses' reports only for demographic data—especially the father's or husband's occupation or education—in order to group families by social class. Some have used individuals' replies about parents to categorize families in terms of political interest or involvement, while others have used respondents' reports of parents' and spouses' voting behavior or partisan attachments. Data about family structure and interaction among family members have been collected perhaps most often by psychologists. Increasingly, however, political scientists have turned to this type of data to study the family influence process (Langton, 1969, chap. 2; Lane, 1969).

The widespread reliance on respondents' reports of family-level data and the unavailability of adequate, general purpose alternatives are persuasive arguments in favor of the continued use of this method. Convenience does not demonstrate validity, however, and the accuracy of reports about the family has properly come under increased scrutiny in recent research.

The extent to which the validity of family-level data has been questioned and the types of issues that have been raised vary with the kind of information under consideration. With factual or "hard" data, it is usually assumed that children's and spouses' reports are "reasonably" accurate. That is, some error is bound to occur, but the reports are accurate enough to be used as actual indicators of parents', spouses', or families' characteristics. This is the assumption, for example, that is implicit in much work that relies on reports of the father's occupation or education to classify children by social backgrounds. The types of errors that might enter into reports of these data have not been specified and the possibility of response bias has usually been ignored. In chapter 2 this assumption of accuracy will be tested by comparing youths' reports of parental characteristics with the parents' own reports. Husbands' and wives' reports will be compared in chapter 4.

Reports of parents' and spouses' voting behavior and political attitudes are somewhat more suspect than those of demographic information. One particular kind of potential bias has been cited most frequently. This can be labeled "self-directed bias," since it is bias that makes others' attitudes or behavior more congruent with one's own preferences or feelings. The effect of this bias on assessing the congruency of parent and student and of husband and wife preferences and attitudes will be one of the major goals of chapters 3 and 5, respectively. However, several other potential sources of reporting errors will also be examined. The questions raised about youths' reports of parental political attributes will also motivate the analysis in chapter 4 of parents' reports about their children's partisan attitudes.

The validity of family-level data has been questioned most frequently and most seriously with regard to reports of family structure and relationships among family members. It has been charged that both children and parents, but especially the latter, bias their responses to make themselves and their families appear more socially acceptable. Moreover, it has been suggested that different members of a family often present varying accounts of the same phenomenon, so that the descriptions of any single member cannot be relied upon. Previous studies, which have leveled these charges or presented data relevant to them, will be reviewed in chapter 5.

It is not surprising that the problem of validity is greatest for reports of family structure and relationships. These characteristics, in contrast to demographic information, yield interpretive or "soft" data. That is, reports of family structure and interaction depend to some extent on individual judgment and interpretation. There are no precise standards by which to determine, say, whether a household is mother- or father-dominated. In fact, there is one point of view which says that there is no such thing as "real" family attributes and that one necessarily deals with each member's varying perceptions of those attributes. The nature of family structure data and the existence of the view that perceptions are more important than real characteristics cause some complex problems involving the assumptions underlying the analysis of these data, the vocabulary used in treating them, and the interpretation of the findings. These problems will be considered in chapters 5 and 8.[4]

STUDY DESIGN

The data to be employed come from a study conducted by the Survey Research Center (SRC) of the University of Michigan in the spring of 1965. Interviews were held with a national probability sample of 1,669 seniors distributed among ninety-seven schools. The student sample is representative of all high school seniors in the continental United States attending a school with a senior class of at least ten students. Schools were selected on the basis of a multistage area probability sample that was stratified with a number of controls and clustered geographically.[5] Controls were also employed to insure proper representation of students in public and nonpublic institutions. Schools were chosen with a probability proportionate to their size. Within each school a systematic random

4. The relative "hardness" of the data also accounts for the placement of certain topics. The number of children in the family, although obviously a part of family structure, is grouped with the other demographic variables because of its factual nature. Questions about husband-wife agreement on politics are included with the variables on family relationships despite their manifest content.

5. Of the original 98 schools, 85 (87%) agreed to participate; attempts to obtain matched substitutes for the refusals resulted in a final total of 97 out of 111 schools contacted (87%).

sample of fifteen to twenty-one students was drawn from a list of all seniors.[6] The response rate for students was 99 percent.

Parents were chosen after the student sample had been selected. For a random third of the students the father was designated for interviewing, for another random third the mother was designated, and for the other third both parents were assigned. In the permanent absence of the designated parent, the other parent or a parent surrogate was interviewed. Interviews were actually completed with at least one parent of 94 percent of the students and with both parents of 26 percent of the students, or 1,992 parents altogether. Among parents the response rate was 93 percent.[7]

Several features of the student and parent samples should be underscored. First, since the sample of students was drawn from a universe of twelfth graders, school dropouts in that age cohort, estimated at around 26 percent for this time period, were automatically eliminated. Second, due mainly to the fact that more mothers than fathers constitute the head of household in single-parent families, the sample of parents is composed of 56 percent mothers. A third point is that most parents are in a relatively restricted age range (35–55). Moreover, most have been married for close to twenty years or more. Wherever possible, I will take these factors into account in both the discussion and analysis.

In part 1, the basic procedure is to match up the student and parent samples so that student-parent pairs are formed. Although the actual number of students for whom we had at least one parent respondent is 1,562, the base number of pairs used in the analysis is 1,992. In order to make maximum usage of the interviews gathered, the paired cases in which both the mother and father were interviewed (430) are each given half of their full value.[8] A further

6. The exact number of students to be chosen was determined by the sampling procedure. Limitations on the minimum size of the senior class and on the range in the number of students within each school were determined so that schools as well as students could be the unit of analysis.

7. Additional interviews were conducted with 317 of the students' most relevant social studies teachers and with the school principals. Some 21,000 paper-pencil questionnaires were administered to all members of the senior class in 85 percent of the sample schools.

8. The alternative to half-weighting these pairs is to subselect among those cases where both mother and father were interviewed. Half-weighting tends to reduce the sampling variability because it utilizes more data cases.

adjustment in weighting, due to unavoidably imprecise estimates at the time the sampling frame was constructed, results in a weighted total of 1,927 parent-student pairs.[9] Occasionally, when I wish to use both the mother's and father's reports, the 430 cases of two-parent interviews will be used.

Another part of the analysis will compare aggregate student and parent responses. For those comparisons, the decision was made to exclude the students for whom parent interviews were not obtained (6 percent of the total student sample). We did not want to find (or mask) differences solely because of the failure to interview some parents. For the same reason, if a student fell out of a particular comparison because his response was not ascertained, the parent was also eliminated, and vice versa. Thus the aggregate comparisons in part 1 are always based on a set of students and on a parent of each (or two parents, each half-weighted). In any case, comparison of the entire student sample and the set of students for whom parents were interviewed showed that differences in any category were invariably less than 1 percent.

Part 2 relies on the 430 husband-wife pairs. The weighted N, due to the adjustments for imprecise estimates described above, is 531. Aggregate comparisons in part 2 are based on the 531 (weighted) wives and the same number of husbands who form the pairs. We could have drawn from the larger pool of husbands and of wives for this part of the analysis, but again it was important that the comparisons not be invalidated by the failure (by design or otherwise) to interview both the husband and wife.

9. It proved impossible to obtain accurate, recent figures on twelfth grade enrollment throughout the country. Working with the data available and extrapolating as necessary, a sampling frame was constructed so that schools would be drawn with a probability proportionate to the size of the senior class. After entry was obtained into the sample schools and precise figures on enrollments gathered, differential weights were applied to correct for the inequalities in selection probabilities occasioned by the original imprecise information. The average weight is 1.2. When the number of cases is cited in text or tables, it will always be a weighted frequency. This is done so that if the reader wishes to recompute percentages (e.g., to combine categories), the correct base will be available. Though noninteger weights were used in the analysis, numbers are rounded for purposes of presentation. On rare occasions this results in minor discrepancies; e.g., a table could show a figure of 28% based on 4 cases because the actual fraction was 1.1/3.9 cases.

The use of high school seniors as the youth sample has some definite implications for the degree of accuracy that will be observed in student and parent reports. This is especially apparent for reports about parents' demographic characteristics and feelings about politics. Compared to other age groups, the seniors may be in the best position to give accurate reports. For a number of reasons —their concern with their own educational and occupational plans, their proximity to full citizenship, and school-generated interest in political matters—high school seniors' reports about these topics are probably markedly better than those of younger children. At the same time, immediately after their high school years, most persons leave the family environment for college, for full-time jobs, for military service, or for establishment of their own families. Removed from day-to-day interaction with their parents, it is unlikely that knowledge about their parents will grow. Although in some instances there is increased interchange about politics as the students move into the active electorate, any improved perceptions about family politics in these cases are probably more than offset by the deteriorating perceptions of many others. Thus the reports of seniors are likely to be at least as accurate as those of older respondents. Parents' reports of the partisan attitudes of their children are likely to be much better for seniors than for younger children, but a full awareness may await the students' adult years.

The effects of using seniors to report family structure and relationships among family members are much less clear. On the one hand, it seems likely that parents' views will be at least as congruent with seniors' views as with those of younger children since seniors have had more years of experience in the family. On the other hand, the teenage years, in which children begin to develop their own views of life, may lead to conflicting perceptions in parents and youths.

The effect of the particular sample of husbands and wives is most likely to increase the congruency of their reports, due to the length of their marriages. While this is something of a handicap for analyzing demographic and political reports (as it may overestimate accuracy rates found elsewhere), it is an advantage for looking at reports of family features (where we will find that agreement is low even among these respondents).

The limitations of the samples are apparent from these considerations. Only by inference can we discuss the validity of reports from young children, or from young couples, or the validity of recall by adults about their childhood experiences. The latter is particularly important since we so often want to know the background of adult samples.

Nevertheless, we can accurately determine the validity of reports received from students approaching the age of full citizenship as well as from middle-aged couples and can establish some worthwhile benchmarks for future studies using different age groups. The use of American students sets another limit on the generalizability of our findings since some cultural differences have been found in the area we are investigating (Converse and Dupeux, 1962, pp. 11–14). Again my goal is to establish some guidelines that can be refined by future studies.

It should be mentioned that the student and parent interviews, which averaged over an hour in length, were designed to cover a wide array of topics, many of which are not used in this book (e.g., the students' social studies courses). Comparison of student and parent and of husband and wife was planned as an integral part of the study, but the resources that could be devoted to it had to be adjusted to fit the needs of the overall investigation.[10] This accounts for the limited variety of subjects (in particular, expressly political matters) on which students and parents were asked about each other. It also explains the occasional use of somewhat different formats for the student and parent questions.

METHODS OF ANALYSIS

To measure agreement between parents and students and between husbands and wives we rely primarily on rank-order correlations. While the obvious alternative of percentage agreement has an intuitive appeal, it has several drawbacks. Percentage agreement is not based on the total configuration of a matrix but only on the "main diagonal." Thus two tables that are similar in percentage agreement may represent widely differing amounts of agreement if

10. The major substantive report of the study is Jennings and Niemi (1974).

deviations from perfect agreement are considered. Moreover, percentage agreement depends heavily on the number of categories used, so that the degree of parent-student or husband-wife similarity might vary for totally artificial reasons. Correlations are more resistant to changes in the definition of categories. Finally, correlations are based on relative rankings (and intervals in the case of product-moment correlations) rather than on absolute agreement as percentage agreement usually is. That is, if student scores tend to be higher (or lower) than parent scores on a particular variable but the students are ranked similarly to their parents, a high correlation may be obtained with very little perfect agreement.

With one exception I will use a rank-order correlation coefficient developed by Kendall, denoted as τ_b (tau-b).[11] This choice was made because almost all of our data are ordinal level. Recently the practice has spread of using interval level statistics for ordinal data. While I am in general sympathetic to this use, the last word on this practice is far from spoken. In the meantime, I think it advisable in a book on measurement to adhere to a statistic designed for the level of measurement actually obtained. In the one instance in which an attempt is made to obtain a close approximation to interval data ("thermometer" ratings of political and social groups, in chapter 7), Pearson product-moment correlations are used.[12]

The tau-b correlation was chosen because it is quite frequently used and is relatively invariant to changes in the number of categories. Most important, however, is that it more closely approximates our usual sense of "agreement" than its chief rival, Goodman and Kruskal's gamma. Gamma is increased by "scalar" relationships, most notably in small tables, and dramatically in 2 × 2 tables. Thus a fourfold table as shown here is a perfect gamma even though 80/100 cases show disagreement about whether the response is an A or a B. In contrast, tau-b is perfect only when all

11. It is also referred to as "tau beta" or as "Kendall's tau corrected for ties." See Blalock (1960, pp. 319–21); on the terminology, see Niemi (1968).
12. Fortunately the relationships among different types of statistics are gradually becoming known. See, for example, Rutherford (1971) and Weisberg (1974).

	A	B
A	10	80
B	0	10

cases lie on one diagonal. Since this corresponds to our usual sense of "agreement" or "accuracy" of alternative responses, tau-*b* seems most appropriate.[13]

Other measures of agreement could have been used, and undoubtedly no single measure will satisfy everyone. Partly in response to this, close attention has been paid to such things as the marginals (which affect the values of measures of agreement that can be obtained) and to agreement within the individual response categories. In addition, whole tables are presented often enough to permit readers to calculate their own measures when some other measure is preferable for a particular purpose.

13. A minor wrinkle is added if all cases lie on one diagonal but not on the "main" diagonal. This is still a perfect tau-*b*—and I would regard it as perfect agreement of a kind—although it would surely be important to point out the nature of the agreement. In practice, this type of agreement rarely occurs.

PART ONE

COMPARISON AND EVALUATION OF STUDENTS' AND PARENTS' REPORTS ABOUT THE FAMILY AND EACH OTHER

2: Students' Reports of Background Information about Their Parents and Families

Demographic or background information collected from respondents—including the father's occupation, mother's and father's education, family composition, income, religion, ethnic background, etc.—is more widely used in political socialization and related studies than any other type of data. Admittedly, family backgrounds are seldom the focal point of analysis, but they do serve several important purposes. At times they are treated as explanatory variables. More often they provide important controls for testing whether observed relationships are due to the social origins of respondents. At other times they are used to detect interaction effects between social origins and other analytic variables. Whatever the purpose, the widespread use of demographic data based on respondents' reports about their parents and families demands at least brief consideration of their validity.

NATURE OF THE DATA

The nature of demographic data makes this a most suitable topic to begin our analysis. In the first place, there are almost always unique, correct answers to questions about background information. Unusual situations occasionally cause problems (e.g., a man with no formal schooling who is obviously "well educated"), but for the most part there is one definite, correct answer.

A second important feature of demographic data is that it can usually be assumed that the reports given by parents (about themselves) are correct. It is true that studies of response validity have shown that some "factual" information is poorly reported by respondents. However, these studies have typically dealt with economic matters (balances in savings accounts, outstanding loans,

17

etc.), medical histories (periods and purposes of hospitalization, recent illnesses, etc.), political behavior (especially voting), and child rearing (for example, ages at which children did certain things).[1] All of these matters are less pervasive, more sensitive, and more transient than background variables. Thus it is quite reasonable to assume that the information provided by parents is correct.[2]

Once this assumption is made, it is possible to speak of the "accuracy" of students' reports (as opposed simply to student-parent "agreement"). This does not mean, however, that all cases in which the student and parent reports differ are necessarily due to poor reporting by the students. Certainly there is some error in the reports given by parents, although it is impossible to say just how much. Another important source of discrepancies, which can be roughly measured, is interviewer and coding error. This will be most obvious when comparing student and parent reports of the number of children in the family. It is hard to imagine that some children are literally forgotten, so that discrepancies in the reports can nearly all be attributed to errors of interviewers and coders. Moreover, an exception to the assumption of parental accuracy will be made for reports of the length of residence in the local community. Ambiguity in the questions used, to be noted below, suggests that students' and parents' responses should be considered about equally accurate.

Note that when applied to personal features, the assumption of parental accuracy will be taken to mean that an individual gives accurate reports of his *own* characteristics. Although husbands and wives give highly accurate reports about each other's job and schooling (see chapter 6), spouses' reports will not be used here. This means that in assessing the accuracy of students' reports of the father's education and occupation, only student-father pairs will

1. For investigations of response error in reporting economic variables, see Lansing et al. (1961), Hauck and Steinkamp (1964), Ferber (1966); for medical data, see Cannell (1965), Cannell and Fowler (1963); for voting, see Clausen (1968–69); and for child rearing, see Wenar (1961), Chess et al. (1960), Goddard et al. (1961).

2. Haberman and Sheinberg (1966) found surprisingly large numbers of discrepancies in reports of education in two waves of a panel study. But the errors were mostly very minor, and some can be attributed to the failure to distinguish between college and noncollege training as was done with the parents in this study (see below).

be used. Only student-mother pairs will be used to check the seniors' reports of their mother's education.

While it can safely be assumed that respondents give accurate demographic information about themselves, the ability of individuals to provide this information about their parents and families is open to question. For one thing, the accuracy of childrens' reports of the parents' occupation and education is undoubtedly a function of age. A minimal amount of information about the father's occupation could be gathered from very young children—for example, whether the father wears overalls or a tie to work. As children grow older, their information about the father's job becomes more extensive and more reliable (Vaillancourt, 1972, p. 50). Children's knowledge of parents' education must begin at a later stage than occupational information and grow at a slower rate.[3] As with job information, it probably begins with gross distinctions between "a lot" of education and "not so much."

Whatever the ages at which educational and occupational information becomes widespread and reasonably detailed, it is likely that a plateau has been reached by the last year of high school. For a number of reasons discussed in chapter 1, reports from seniors are probably more accurate than those from any other age group. The test in this chapter, then, will be of a minimal sort. To the extent that the students' reports are highly accurate, it confirms our expectations for this cohort, leaving open the question of the adequacy of reports from other age groups. Nevertheless, even this minimal confirmation has been missing heretofore. Moreover, if the seniors cannot provide accurate information, it is unlikely that younger children could do so. Finally, variations in the accuracy of reports will allow us to specify some of the conditions underlying accurate and inaccurate reporting.

Questions Used in This Study

The principal demographic variables to be studied in this chapter are the father's occupation and the father's and mother's education.

---

3. Douvan and Adelson (1966, p. 318) report that boys, ages 14–16, and girls, ages 11–17, were almost all able to report their father's occupation, while 13% could not report the father's education. See also Coleman et al. (1966, p. 570).

These variables were chosen, at the time of questionnaire construction, because they are the most frequently used items of background information. The main questions on occupation were straightforward and identical for parent and student samples:

> *What is your (your father's) occupation? I mean, what kind of work do you (does he) do? (If not clear or obvious) What exactly do you (does he) do on your (his) job? What kind of business is that?*

Interviewers were instructed to probe for complete responses. For the parents, an additional question asked whether the respondent worked for himself or someone else, and questions were included for those who were unemployed or retired.[4] In another part of the interview, students were also asked what occupation they hoped to follow after they finished their education.

Two occupation codes and an industry code were used to record the responses. The first occupation code is the detailed classification of 500 occupations used in the 1950 Census of Population. Assigned to each of these occupations is a socioeconomic index score (SES), ranging from 1 to 99. These scores, developed by O. D. Duncan on the basis of census data, represent a linear combination of the average income and education of employed males falling into each occupational category. The linear combination was determined by using a multiple regression equation to predict the prestige scores given each occupation in a National Opinion Research Center nationwide cross-section sample. The SES index was then used to divide one meaningful population—the male labor force in 1960—into deciles. Note that although each decile by definition contains (approximately) 10 percent of that population, some deciles contain many occupations and a wide range of the SES scores, while others cover few jobs and a narrow band of SES scores. For some purposes (for example, as it is used below to determine mobility), it seems more appropriate to use the decile scores than SES scores. With the latter, a small difference in scores in some ranges indicates considerable movement in terms of the overall distribution of the population, whereas in other ranges a

4. *Do you work for yourself or someone else? What kind of work do you usually do? What kind of work did you do before you retired?*

large difference indicates little or no change in the decile in which one is classified.[5]

The second occupation code is a moderately detailed list of about 40 categories, which was developed for the Survey Research Center. Usually, seven major classifications will be used, as described below. Finally, the fathers were classified in a ten-category industry code. This code is based not on the respondent's specific job but on the industry in which he works. It requires information about the types of business in which one is employed and may not be given as readily by respondents unless probing is used.[6]

The father's and the mother's educations were tapped, in the parent interview, by a series of questions developed for earlier SRC studies. The full set of questions is given, although only part of the information will be used here:

> *How many grades of school did you finish?*
> (If more than eight) *Have you had any other schooling?* (If yes)
> *What other schooling have you had?*
> (If attended college) *What colleges did you attend? Where is that located? What was your college major? Do you have a college degree?* (If yes) *What degree(s) did you receive? At what college did you get your (highest) degree?*

The information gained from these questions permits detailed coding. The exact number of grades completed is coded through grade twelve. Additional codes provide for noncollege training, some college, and bachelor's, master's, and doctor's degrees. Specific colleges and college majors were coded and will be used in chapter 6. In contrast to this carefully constructed set of questions, one simple question was adopted for the student interviews. The seniors were asked simply: *How far did your father go in school? How far did your mother go?*

---

5. For details about these scores, see the chapters by Duncan in Reiss (1961).

6. The 10 categories are as follows: agriculture and agricultural services, 5 categories of private business (mining, construction, forestry; manufacturing; transportation and utilities; wholesale trade; retail sales), 3 categories of services (services primarily to business; personal, repair, and recreation services primarily to the public; professional services to the public), and government.

Besides inquiring about the number of children in the family, we asked students and parents only one other question of a demographic nature: *How long have you lived in the (name of community) area?* Each interviewer filled in the proper community name. They were instructed to refer to the specific locality if the respondent lived in a metropolitan area. Unquestionably, there is room for ambiguity here. Although in many cases the same person interviewed a student and his parent, there is no assurance that the same community name was always used. In any case, the bounds of a community are not always fixed so firmly in people's minds as on city maps.[7]

INDIVIDUAL COMPARISONS

In this chapter even the briefest comparison of aggregate or group comparisons can be dispensed with. For all of the variables, only trivial differences appear between the proportion of student and parent responses in any category.[8] The one issue that should be touched on at the aggregate level, before turning directly to a comparison of student-parent pairs, is the number of cases in which background information was not provided. For this age cohort, "don't know" responses are negligible. They constitute less than 1 percent of the student responses, even for the mother's education. A more important practical problem is the existence of some homes in which a parent is permanently absent due to death, divorce, or separation. There are few homes in which the mother is absent (about 2 percent), but about 10 percent of the homes are without a father. In most instances, information about the absent parent is missing, although occasionally it was supplied by the student. These cases will not adversely affect the student accuracy rates described below, because the rates are necessarily based only on those cases in which a parent was actually interviewed.[9]

7. Despite the obvious nature of this problem, there is no simple way around it. For an analytic use of geographic mobility, based on a question similar to that used here, see Douvan and Adelson (1966, pp. 336–38).

8. The only exceptions to this statement are for the education categories "12 grades" and "12 grades plus noncollege school." This will be discussed in the section on accuracy within specific categories.

9. However, the fact that information about the father is missing for about 10% of a sample of this age group suggests that more than one item

When background information is supplied by students, it appears to be very accurate. Figure 2.1 presents the basic correlations. The top and bottom items are based on all-parent pairs, while the other items involve student-father or student-mother pairs. Each of the correlations is based on a large number of categories—the exact number of children, eight categories of education, seven occupation

.92	Number of children in the family
.80	Father's education
.76	Mother's education
.74	Father's occupation (SRC code)
.70	Father's occupation (Duncan decile code)
.61	Length of residence in the community

Figure 2.1
Tau-*b* Correlations between Student and Parent
Reports of Demographic Variables

groups, and nine categories of length of residence (grouped into two-year periods).[10] Tables 2.1 and 2.2 compare, in percentage

---

of background information should be collected or at least that provisions should be made to substitute an item when the first one is unavailable (e.g., the mother's education in place of the father's when the father is absent). This would remove the possibility that as many as 10% of the cases would have to be deleted from analyses using family background material.

10. Parents who had lived in the same community for 16 or more years were collapsed into one category that was equated with the student response of "all my life."

Table 2.1
Student and Father Reports of Father's Education
(In percentages; N = 1,047)

Father's Report

Student's Report	0–7 grades	8 grades	9–11 grades	12 grades	12 grades and noncollege school	Some college	Bachelor's degree	Advanced degree	Total[a]
0–7 grades	7	1	1	*	0	*	0	0	10
8 grades	2	8	2	*	0	0	0	0	13
9–11 grades	1	3	11	3	2	1	*	0	21
12 grades	*	1	3	14	6	2	*	0	26
12 grades and noncollege school	0	0	*	1	2	1	0	*	3
Some college	0	0	*	0	1	10	1	1	13
Bachelor's degree	0	0	0	0	*	1	6	5	9
Advanced degree	0	0	0	0	0	*	1	6	5
Total[a]	10	13	18	19	11	15	9	6	100

* Less than 1%.
[a] Marginal totals may differ from sums of rows or columns due to rounding.

Table 2.2
Student and Father Reports of Father's Occupation
(In percentages; N = 904[a])

Father's Report

Student's Report	Profes-sional and technical	Self-employed businessmen, managers and officials	Clerical and sales	Skilled workers	Semi-skilled operatives and kindred workers	Service workers	Unskilled laborers	Total[a]
Professional and technical	12	1	1	1	*	0	0	15
Self-employed businessmen, managers and officials	2	17	1	1	*	*	*	21
Clerical and sales	*	3	8	1	1	0	0	12
Skilled workers	1	2	*	19	2	*	*	25
Semi-skilled operatives and kindred workers	*	*	*	2	11	*	1	16
Service workers	*	*	*	*	*	6	*	7
Unskilled laborers	0	0	*	1	1	*	1	4
Total[b]	15	24	11	26	16	6	3	100

* Less than 1%.
[a] The number of cases is smaller than for reports of the father's education because retirees and all farm occupations are removed and because more responses were "NA" (not ascertained).
[b] Marginal totals may differ from sums of rows and columns due to rounding.

form, the reports of students and fathers about the latter's education and occupation.[11] The table comparing reports of the mother's education (not shown) is very similar to that shown for fathers.

The relative positions of the extreme items in figure 2.1 hardly need to be explained. It should be mentioned, however, that the relatively low correlation for the length of local residency is not due to minor disagreements of only a year or two (which could easily be due to rounding). First of all, the reports were grouped into two-year periods; moreover, such minor differences would not lower the correlation very much. This emphasizes the need to clarify community bounds and to find ways to reduce reporting errors by both parents and students.[12]

The middle items in figure 2.1—occupation and education—have quite similar correlations. There is little basis in terms of their reliability for advising use of one rather than the other measure for this cohort. While the statistic is slightly larger for education (at least the father's), this is partly a function of the categories chosen.[13] A simple index, which combined both background factors, yielded a correlation of .78, that is, between the correlations for each factor by itself.[14] Such an index might still be worthwhile from

11. All fathers with farm occupations (7% of the total) are eliminated here. They will be treated at length below.

12. One helpful procedure is to ask respondents to give specific dates rather than number of years.

13. While the tau-b correlation is relatively insensitive to changes in the definition of categories, it is not immovable. Collapsing education into "grade school," "high school," and "college" categories and the SRC occupation codes into white collar and blue collar results in the following correlations: father's education .82, mother's education .78, father's occupation .80.

14. The index was constructed by cross-tabulating occupation and education as follows:

		Education				
Code	1	2	3	$\cdots$		8
1	1	2	3			8
2	2	3	4	$\cdots$		9
Occupation　3	3	4	5			10
$\vdots$		$\vdots$				
7	7	8	9			14

Collapsing was done to make 9 approximately equal categories.

a theoretical point of view. It does depend on two background components and does result in changes in the relative ranking of some individuals. But in terms of the validity of using student responses as a substitute for parental reports, the individual items or the combined items are about equal.

The high correlations obtained here should not obscure the fact that students' and parents' responses often differ in their precise categorization. Comparing reports of parental education *in their full codes,* we see that 51 percent of the students and mothers and 48 percent of the students and fathers show exact agreement. For occupation, students' and fathers' responses were compared on the full list of 500 census categories, with a similar result. Fifty-two percent of the student reports were coded in exactly the same category as their fathers' reports. These results may seem to contradict the high agreement rates indicated by the correlations based on these data, but as indicated in chapter 1, percentage agreement takes no account of the magnitude of disagreement, so that minor errors (e.g., student says eleventh grade, father says tenth grade) are given the same weight as major errors. The proportion of cases with exact agreement does have the heuristic value of showing that some loss of precision is involved in using student rather than parent reports.[15] For most purposes, however, such a high degree of precision is unnecessary. Much more important are the possibilities of bias in student responses or the existence of certain systematic errors that make student reports unreliable for specified segments of the population. These subjects are taken up next.

Bias in Students' Responses

In later chapters on family characteristics, responses of students and parents will be examined for bias in socially acceptable directions. For students' reports of demographic data, an analogous kind of bias is overreporting of high prestige occupations and overestimating the parent's educational achievements. This type of bias is much less likely for factual information than for reports of more

---

15. It is certainly true that some errors occur in parent reports if precise categorization is used. However, it is still safe to assume that the parents' reports are more accurate than the students'.

subjective matters. The psychological processes underlying biased reports of family characteristics may be very subtle, and respondents are probably unaware that their reports are in any sense false or misleading. With factual data it is less likely that respondents could unwittingly give biased reports—at least for salient topics such as education and occupation. A large amount of bias would require that students consciously misreported their family backgrounds. A more plausible hypothesis is that errors in reporting factual matters are due to a variety of causes, some of which result in overestimating family status and others which result in underestimating it. Due to these crosscutting effects, no bias will appear.

Comparison of student and parent reports of the father's occupation and the parents' education support the latter hypothesis. One comparison of occupational reports can be derived directly from table 2.2. Fifteen percent of the student reports of the father's occupation are coded in a higher category than the father's own report. Nearly as many students, 11 percent, report the father's job as being lower in status than it is. A second comparison, using the decile scale from the Duncan code, also shows a small difference, but with a narrow majority underestimating the status of the father's job. In 20 percent of the cases the student's report is in a lower decile than the father's, while it is in a higher decile 16 percent of the time. The educational comparisons likewise reveal no bias. Fourteen percent of the students report the father's education as being higher than it is, but 17 percent underestimate his training.[16] Nearly equal proportions of the students overestimate the mother's education (15 percent) and underestimate it (14 percent). In short, a comparison of student and parent reports for the entire sample shows no discernible tendency for students to bias the background information they provide. If it is not accurate, it is just as likely to lower as to raise the prestige or status of the parent.

16. The latter figure, derived from table 2.1, does not count an additional 6% of the students who underestimated the father's education by failing to report the noncollege education of the fathers. For the same reason 6% of the reports of the mother's education were not counted. It would be misleading to consider these reports as biased, since the parents but not the students were asked about noncollege training. This will be discussed in detail later.

Despite the finding of no bias for the sample as a whole, one might suspect that there are actually multiple biases that affect different segments of the population in such a way as to effectively cancel one another when the total sample is observed. Specifically, people who are upwardly mobile may overestimate the prestige of the father's occupation and the parents' educational achievements, while downwardly mobile individuals may underestimate the parents' prestige and accomplishments. For upwardly mobile individuals, this would have the advantage of masking their lower-status origins, which mark them as new arrivals at a given social level. Downwardly mobile persons would be served by lowering the prestige of their family background, since it would tend to obscure their descent.

Since many of the seniors in the study sample would not end their education with graduation, and since virtually none had begun his lifetime work, mobility can be determined only by classifying students according to their intentions. Responses to questions about a student's future occupational plans were compared with his parent's occupation and education. For boys only, occupational mobility was determined by comparing the decile code of the student's (intended) occupation with the decile code of the father's occupation, as reported by the father. If the decile code for the student's occupation was lower than that for his father's job, the student was considered downwardly mobile. Two categories of upward mobility were formed by students whose chosen occupation ranked one or two deciles above the father's and three or more deciles above it. When the decile scores matched, the student was status stable. Ceiling and ground limitations were operative, of course, so that students from high-status families could not be upwardly mobile or students from low-status families downwardly mobile. An education mobility index was created by comparing a student's educational intentions with the education of his mother (when the reports of the mother's education were to be examined) or his father (when the father's education was to be studied). If the student planned no education beyond high school, he was considered downwardly mobile, stable, or upwardly mobile depending on whether his parent's education was less than twelve years, ex-

actly twelve years, or more. Students planning on noncollege training and those planning college education were divided into the
same three groups in a similar manner.

Within these mobility groups, student and parent reports of the
parent's education and occupation were again compared (using
the SRC occupation categories). The results *seem* to support the
hypothesis of multiple biases that counteract one another in the
total sample. The figures for occupational mobility are typical.
Among downwardly mobile students who incorrectly reported the
father's occupation, 66 percent reported an occupation which is
lower in prestige than that given by the father. Of the status-stable
students, 67 percent reported a lower prestige occupation, while
among the upwardly mobile groups, 52 percent and 39 percent reported lower prestige jobs. These results are not perfect, for the
status-stable group did not split evenly between raising and lowering the father's prestige, and only among the high upwardly mobile
students did a majority raise the father's prestige. But there is a
rather consistent pattern that alters the apparent social origins of
the various mobility groups.

This evidence, however, is subject to varying interpretations.
On the one hand, it is doubtful that this bias is the result of deliberate misreporting by students. With another purpose in mind,
a comparison was made (directly from the protocols) of 120 pairs
of interviews in which the student and parent gave different reports of the father's occupation. In only a few cases was there a
clear-cut discrepancy, in which the occupation reported by the
student and parent bore little resemblance to each other. Many of
the differences occurred because of slight variations in the wording
of student and parent responses or because the student failed to
report some aspect of the father's occupation, such as that he
worked for himself or that he had some supervisory responsibilities.
Even if students wanted to bias their reports, it is unlikely that they
could do so by slight alterations in wording or by deliberate omis-
sion of selected information.

A more important consideration than a lack of desire or ability
by students to bias their reports is that dividing the students into
mobility groups necessarily affects the distribution of occupational

or educational types in each group. The distribution in turn influences the proportion of students who overestimate and underestimate their parents' prestige and accomplishments. For example, upwardly mobile sons have fathers with low-status occupations much more than the total cross section and rarely if ever have fathers with high-status jobs (because of ceiling effects). If these upwardly mobile students report the father's occupation inaccurately, they are more likely to overestimate the status of the father's job even if there is no intentional bias in that direction. This is revealed by an examination of the types of reporting errors made for each occupational category. Mentally percentaging down the columns in table 2.2 shows that students overestimate the father's status more often when the father has a low-status job.[17] For the lowest category, of course, erroneous reports can be in only one direction. Since upwardly mobile students have parents who are heavily clustered in low-status jobs, their reports are weighted with overestimates of the father's status to a greater extent than for the total sample of students. Just the opposite effect can be observed among downwardly mobile students. Therefore, the bias observed among mobility groups is almost totally artifactual and probably reflects very little in the way of intentional misrepresentation of the students' background.

This interpretation, while perhaps valid, is totally irrelevant from another point of view. While it may be important that the bias is not due to intentional misreporting, the bias is still present and may have undesirable consequences. If, for example, one analyzes a sample or subsample of students who are relatively homogeneous with respect to mobility, the distribution of the parents' occupation or education may be poorly estimated by the students' reports. To some extent this viewpoint is correct, since marginal distributions are indeed affected by the bias found in mobility groups. But the effect is small because the amount of bias is not too great and

17. A major contributing factor to this pattern may simply be coding error. For all categories except the middle one, there is an unequal number of cells indicating higher and lower prestige. If coding errors are randomly distributed, the distribution of inaccurate reports will be directly related to the number of each type of cell.

mainly because it is superimposed on a large complement of accurate reports. Illustratively, two sets of distributions are given in table 2.3, one for students who are highly upwardly mobile in occupation and the other for students who are downwardly mobile in education. These distributions were selected because they yielded the greatest differences in marginals of all the cases observed. The

Table 2.3
Student and Father Reports of Father's Occupation
and Education, in Two Mobility Groups
(In percentages)

Students Highly Upwardly Mobile in Intended Occupation (N = 111)			Students Downwardly Mobile in Intended Education (N = 94)		
Father's occupation	*Father's reports*	*Student's reports*	Father's education	*Father's reports*	*Student's reports*
Self-employed businessmen, managers and officials	8	12	0–8 grades	0	1
Clerical and sales	5	4	9–11 grades	0	7
			12 grades/12 grades and noncollege		
Skilled workers	35	34	school	20	25
Semi-skilled operatives and kindred workers	34	34	Some college	52	40
Service workers	8	7	Bachelor's degree	21	21
Unskilled			Advanced		
laborers	10	9	degree	7	6
Total	100	100	Total	100	100

NOTE: Operational definitions of the mobility groups are given in the text.

bias is reflected in the overestimate of high-status occupations and underestimate of educational achievements in the student as compared with the parent reports. That the effect of the bias is no larger than this for the "worst" cases suggests that the use of students' reports will not invalidate studies based on homogeneous mobility groups.

A second consequence of the bias in students' reports is that the determination of mobility groups will itself be affected by the use of students' rather than parents' reports of parental background. Some students report their parent's job or education as higher or lower status than it actually is, and their relative mobility may be judged differently if students' rather than parents' reports are used to determine mobility groups. There is some validity to this argument; a few individuals are judged differently when student rather than parent reports are used. But 80 percent or more of the students are rated exactly the same whichever reports are utilized. The correlations between mobility as determined by student and by parent reports are .80 for occupation, .76 for father's education, and .76 for mother's education. Thus the mobility groups will be largely the same regardless of which report is used.

Other consequences of the bias observed in students' reports could be mentioned, and it is impossible to show that the effects will never be significant. The fact is, however, that a large majority of the students' reports are accurate—even among the highly mobile —and that the amount of bias is not too great. In general, then, analyses based on homogeneous mobility groups are not likely to be hampered by the bias in student reports. When analyses are based on more heterogeneous samples, the likelihood of error due to this bias is certainly negligible.

One other type of potential bias should be mentioned here since it will be important in later chapters. It is plausible that students bias their perceptions of one parent in the direction of the other one. As a consequence, parents would be made to appear more similar than they really are. It turns out that no such tendency is observable for reports of demographic data. In fact, using the 430 families in which both parents were interviewed, we find that the student reports yield a correlation of .48 between the mother's and father's education, while the parent reports give a slightly higher value of .54. The report of factual information about one parent did not affect the student's report about the other parent.[18]

18. In addition, the students' reports were equally accurate whether the father and mother had similar or different amounts of education.

Accuracy of Student Reports within Categories of
Education and Occupation

So far no mention has been made of variations in the accuracy of students' reports depending on the education or occupation of the parents. For the most part these variations are relatively small, but they provide a number of worthwhile insights. Table 2.4 gives the percentage of students reporting their father's and mother's education accurately for each education level. The most striking fact

Table 2.4
Accuracy of Student Reports of Parent's Education

| Parent's Education (own report) | Student's Report of Parent's Education | | | |
| | Father | | Mother | |
	Percent accurate	Number of cases	Percent accurate	Number of cases
0–7 grades	68	103	52	96
8 grades	63	141	59	141
9–11 grades	63	184	73	271
12 grades	78	195	76	340
12 grades and noncollege school	15	111	33	205
Some college	63	161	68	139
Bachelor's degree	74	92	82	90
Advanced degree	79	60	58	20
Total	63	1,047	64	1,302

is that the proportion correctly indicating that their parent had finished high school plus noncollege schooling is drastically out of line with the other proportions. Evidently the simple question used in the student interviews failed to elicit this type of schooling, whereas the parent question brought it out.[19] The loss of this information may not be very serious, since it is rarely used to categorize respondents, but it does indicate one type of detailed information lost by using a relatively simple question.

19. The lower percentage of correct answers in this category for the father's than for the mother's education may be because the fathers more often report on-the-job training as well as formal schooling. This type of information might not be reported by the students even if detailed questions were used.

Another feature of the observed variations is that students seem to report their parents' education more accurately if they finished rather than attended only a portion of a particular level of schooling. The mother's education is reported more accurately if she finished elementary school rather than attending grades one through seven; both parents' education is described more faithfully if they graduated from high school or college rather than dropping out. The one reversal occurs among fathers with only an elementary education. Moreover, the percentage of correct reports of high school and college graduates is underestimated because of some vague responses by the students. Answers such as "high school" and "college" were insufficient to distinguish graduates from dropouts. All of these responses were arbitrarily treated as indicating "some" high school or college, although undoubtedly this was not the intent of all the students. Thus when the parent graduated from high school or college, these students appear to give erroneous reports.[20]

The greater proportion of accurate reports among children of graduates can probably be attributed in part to a tendency of students to "round off" their parents' education, similar to the way individuals round off their ages to five-year intervals. Also, some parents may be reluctant to discuss with their children the fact that they began high school or college and then dropped out. In addition, having a diploma or degree adds concreteness to the grade of school completed and no doubt makes others more aware of that attainment. Finally, there are elements of ambiguity in the student questions that may have reduced the accuracy of students' reports when a parent did not finish a given level of education. On the one hand, a few students, especially at the high school level, may have responded that their parent went to twelfth grade or four years of college without noting that the parent did not complete the final year. On the other hand, some students may have neglected to mention that the parent went partially through high school or college because they know the parent did not complete that level. On both

20. For the sample as a whole this is not a serious problem, since only about 4.5% of the responses were this vague. However, it may result in underestimating the proportion of correct responses among children of high school graduates by as much as 15% and among college graduates by as much as 10%.

matters the series of parent questions is very explicit. Thus, some of the apparent reporting errors made by the students are as much a function of the type of question used as of the students' inability to provide the desired information. Although student reports of parental education are very accurate, a detailed set of questions similar to those used in the parent interview would have made them even more accurate.

The reports of the father's occupation also show variations in accuracy that can be attributed partly to the type of questions used rather than to bad reporting by students. The proportion of accurate student reports for various occupations is given in table 2.5.

Table 2.5
Accuracy of Student Reports of Father's Occupation

Father's Occupation (own report)	Student's Report of Father's Occupation	
	Percent accurate	*Number of cases*
Professional and technical	79	135
Self-employed businessmen, managers and officials	69	223
Clerical and sales	74	96
Skilled workers	73	236
Semi-skilled operatives and kindred workers	70	148
Service workers	91	54
Unskilled (nonfarm) laborers	43	26
Farmers and farm laborers	84	78
Total	74	996

All farm occupations—wage laborers, owners and tenants, and managers—are combined here. They will be analyzed separately below. The one category (unskilled laborers) that shows an unusually low accuracy rate will not be treated extensively because it is based on a relatively small number of cases.

Aside from the "unskilled" category just mentioned, the lowest rate of accuracy occurs when the father is in the "self-employed, managers and officials" category. This is especially interesting since it was noted earlier that parents were asked a supplementary question about whether they worked for themselves or for someone else. This allowed proper coding of fathers who neglected to mention in their initial response that they were self-employed. It is possible that some of the errors in students' reports were a direct result of the failure to ask them the extra question. With this in mind, a check was made of all interviews in which the father fell into the "businessman" category while the student's response was coded otherwise. Of these sixty-nine cases, the extra question might have clarified the student's report in twenty-two of them. In all of these twenty-two cases the student's and father's reports were very similar, except that the father stated—either initially or in response to the supplementary question—that he was self-employed, while the student failed to note this. If these reports had been clarified, children with "businessman" fathers would have correctly identified the father's occupation in 79 percent of the cases, an increase of 10 percent. In terms of the overall sample, an additional 2 percent of the students would have given accurate reports.

Use of the supplementary question on self-employment would also have enlightened the coding of farm occupations. Thus far the problem has been sidestepped by treating all types of "farmers" as a single commodity, whereas often some distinctions are made. The most important demarcations are among farm owners and tenants, farm managers, and farm laborers, although the latter group can be broken down further. These distinctions are quite meaningful in terms of socioeconomic status. Most farm laborers are on a par with unskilled nonfarm laborers (in the first decile of the Duncan code), and the SRC code combines these groups under the same general heading. Farm owners and tenants (second decile on the Duncan code) and especially farm managers (seventh decile) are ranked higher. These distinctions were captured reasonably well in the parent questionnaire; the ambiguous response "farmer" was clarified by coding those self-employed as owners or tenants and those who worked for someone else as farm laborers. The absence of this question in the student interview meant that many fathers were classified by the student's report as "farmers, NA what type." For those cases, it could not be determined whether the father was a farm laborer or an owner or tenant.[21] In terms of the sample of parents, of course, the failure to capture

21. It is not suggested that the question on self-employment is ideal for distinguishing all census farm categories—e.g., unpaid family workers—but it would at least distinguish owners and tenants from laborers.

this distinction in the student reports would result in only a small loss of information since all farm occupations made up less than 10 percent of the total. For analyses of specific subgroups such as laborers, the loss would be much more significant. And, in general, it is another illustration of how the type of question affected the apparent accuracy of student responses quite apart from their ability to provide the desired information.

Aside from the reduced accuracy of students' reports imposed by the question forms, the most important observation about the figures in table 2.5 is that accuracy rates are quite similar for all occupational types. There may be a slight tendency for lower accuracy among blue-collar occupations (especially if the percentage for unskilled laborers were approximately correct). However, the differences are not large and, in fact, the blue-collar category of service workers shows the highest accuracy rate of all. Thus, despite the difficulty of distinguishing skilled workers from operatives, and operatives from unskilled laborers, the reporting and coding of blue-collar occupations has been done with about the same skill as for higher-status jobs.

This relative uniformity of accuracy levels is an important supplement to the high accuracy rates for the entire sample. Wide variations in accuracy among the various occupational types would not disturb the overall findings, but they would lend little confidence to analyses based only on the poorly reported occupations. In contrast, the relatively similar degree of accuracy found here means that one can place confidence in analyses based on an entire cross-section sample or on selected occupational groups. Unfortunately, this desirable property of uniform agreement rates will not always be found when we group individuals by sociological characteristics.

Correlates of Accurate Student Reports

The accuracy of student responses might reasonably be expected to vary with a number of personal and family characteristics. First of all, there may be some differences depending on the sex of the student. In particular, boys may be more accurate reporters of the father's occupation. It turns out that boys do give slightly better accounts of their father's job, but the difference is very small. The correlation between student and father reports is .77 for boys and .73 for girls. For reports of parental education the boy-girl difference is reversed, but still small. Correlations for reporting the father's education are .80 for boys and .81 for girls; for the mother's education the corresponding values are .73 and .79. The accuracy rates for length of residence in the local community show little variation for parent-student sex combinations although boys and mothers again reveal the least agreement.[22]

Table 2.6
Tau-*b* Correlations between Student and Parent Reports
of Demographic Variables, by Type of Parent Respondent

Type of Parent Respondent	Variables				
	Number of children	*Father's education*	*Mother's education*	*Father's occupation*	*Length of local residence*
One of two natural parents present	.96	.81	.77	.75	.63
N[a]	1,563	965	1,029	901	1,493
The only natural parent present	.89	.83	.76	.69	.55
N	262	31	230	31	254
Stepparent or parent surrogate[b]	.49	.58	.62	.73	.44
N	98	52	43	63	96

[a] The number of cases for fathers and mothers separately add to more than the number of cases for the total sample because a different weighting procedure is appropriate when controlling for sex of parent.
[b] This category is divided almost equally between stepparents and parent surrogates.

By far the largest variations in accuracy rates occur when the sample is divided on the basis of whether the interview was with a natural parent or a substitute parent.[23] The figures in the first two rows of table 2.6 show that it makes little difference whether the

22. It should also be mentioned that there is no patterned variation in the accuracy of reporting when the student's grade average is used as a control.
23. Not surprisingly, the student reports of whom they live with coincide almost perfectly with the parent reports of the family situation. The few disagreements are probably due to interviewer or coding error or to some highly unusual circumstances.

student lives with both natural parents or only one as long as the interview was conducted with a natural parent. Information about a natural parent in single-parent families or in homes where a re-marriage has taken place is just about as accurate as in natural nuclear families. However, when a stepparent or parent surrogate is the "parent" interviewee, the accuracy of student reports de-creases sharply, except for occupation.

At least two forces are at work here. In some cases the student had lived with a stepparent or surrogate for only a short while and had had little time to learn his new parent's background. Of more fundamental importance, however, is that the introduction of a new parent often makes the questions on family background highly ambiguous. Does the question on father's education refer to the youth's natural father or to the new parent? Or does it depend on how long he has lived with the present parent? Does it make any difference if the youth's current residence is a semipermanent arrangement or only a temporary home? Even the questions on number of children and length of local residency become unclear. Is a youth supposed to report stepbrothers and stepsisters? Is he to report them even if he has never lived with them? Does the length of residence question refer to the youth himself? If so, his new parent may legitimately give a quite different answer.[24]

These examples illustrate the complexity of the situation when the family is reconstituted. In fact, where a surrogate was inter-viewed in place of a natural parent, the correlation between the student's report and that of his parent surrogate is really not a good measure of the accuracy of the student's report. For example, a student may correctly say that his father (meaning his natural father) had an eighth grade education, while the surrogate correctly says that he (meaning himself) graduated from high school. When the two reports are matched, there appears to be an error where there really was none. But this is partly the point. If we do not know to whom the students' reports refer, less confidence can be

24. These questions were handled on an informal basis by the interview-ers, and there is no way of knowing how uniform their procedures were. Interviewer instructions made it clear only that the questions should some-times be asked about parent substitutes.

placed in them. Similar problems arise when the natural nuclear family is broken down in other ways—for example, by a number of students who were married.

These problems—while they may cause nightmares for fastidious coders—should not be overemphasized for most survey sample work. Comparison of the correlations in the top row of table 2.6 with those given in figure 2.1 shows that overall accuracy rates are affected very little by the addition of a small number of ambiguous cases. (Parent surrogates constitute about 5 percent of the parent sample.) Moreover, the impossibility of designing questionnaires or codes to deal with all the idiosyncratic situations that may arise suggests that the problem of broken and reconstructed homes should be handled on an ad hoc basis by interviewers and coders. This may in fact be a reasonable answer when it can be determined beforehand that few unusual situations will arise. But in samples or subsamples where many families are likely to be broken, extra time and effort will be necessary to be sure that information is as accurate as possible.

A partial illustration of the effects of different family types is given by the reduced correlations for black families in the sample.[25] The correlation between student and parent reports of the father's education is .80 for whites and .74 for blacks; for length of residence the corresponding correlations are .62 and .51; and for the number of children the figures are .94 and .76.[26] The lower correlations for blacks are due largely to the presence of a greater number of surrogates who were interviewed in the place of absent fathers. When only natural nuclear families among blacks are considered, the correlations for the number of children (.90) and length of residence (.56) are closer to those for whites, and the statistic for the father's education (.83) is actually higher. In the present case the accuracy rates for blacks are not so low that the student reports must be completely disregarded, but they do show

25. Throughout this book, 12 respondents classified as "nonwhite, other than black" are grouped with the black subsample.
26. Reports of the mother's education were as accurate for blacks as for whites. This is understandable since there are few stepparents or parent surrogates among the women in the black portion of the sample.

the impact of the unusually large number of parent surrogates. In other specially selected samples (perhaps blacks as a whole rather than only families where the child has finished high school), the problems imposed by irregular family patterns would be of a much larger magnitude.

When the correlations between student and parent reports about demographic variables were introduced in figure 2.1, the question was temporarily deferred as to whether the student reports were sufficiently accurate to be relied upon exclusively for information about parental and family background. Having examined the student reports rather intensively, we may now conclude safely that the seniors are in fact excellent reporters of demographic information. This conclusion rests on several considerations besides the high correlations reported initially:

1. No bias was found when the sample as a whole was examined. The bias that was uncovered would occur only in groups that were highly homogeneous with regard to intergenerational mobility. Moreover, the bias is small enough that it would probably have little effect on most analytic efforts.

2. Some of the differences between the reports of students and parents were not due to lack of information or bad reporting by the students.

a. Some loss of accuracy occurred because less detailed education and occupation questions were used in the student interviews. Probably only a small portion of the total number of student reports were wrong because of the simple questions used (perhaps 2 percent for occupation and less for education), but the accuracy of reporting within certain categories of occupation and education was significantly reduced. It was also suggested (although it cannot be proven with the present data) that many of the errors in reporting length of local residence can be attributed to the ambiguity of community boundaries and to reporting errors by parents as well as students.

b. Coding error contributed to apparent inconsistencies. For reporting of occupations, as many as 10 percent of all student reports may have been "wrong" because of coding errors. This figure was estimated from an examination of 120 pairs of interviews in which the student and parent were coded differently.[27] As expected, about equal numbers of errors were made in coding students and parents.

3. Accuracy rates were reasonably high across all categories of occupation and education (or would have been if detailed student questions had been used).

This optimistic conclusion must be tempered by three major caveats. First, although respondents' reports of demographic information about their parents and families are likely to be quite accurate in any case, they can be improved by the use of detailed questions or series of questions. This point has been made earlier. It need only be added here that the decision to opt for extreme accuracy or somewhat less detail in questions about a respondent's background differs little from the decisions that must be made with regard to most survey items. When questions pertain only to the respondent, it is usually possible to design alternative questions that yield different levels of precision. It must be decided whether the accuracy gained by exhaustive questions is worth the high price of leaving out something else.[28] Too often it is felt that this decision need not be made when background information is desired. It is reasoned that since the respondent has less information about others than about himself, less detailed questions should be asked. This thinking is well advised if it cautions against asking respondents questions that are likely to generate nearly random responses (such as the opinion of a friend about some public policy). But for matters on which the respondent is reasonably well informed, we pay the price of accuracy by using imprecise questions. Sometimes it is necessary to forego accuracy in the interest of saving time, but at least the decision should be made knowingly, with an awareness of the possible alternatives and some

27. This does not mean that coding errors were made on 10% of the interviews in each sample. If the errors were approximately randomly distributed across 7 occupational categories, it would seldom happen that the reports of a student and his father both were miscoded but still matched. Therefore, the proportion of student-parent *pairs* in which a coding error would be made is approximately the sum of the percentage of coding errors in each sample.

28. Precise questions are not always long ones, but this is often the case. They frequently have screening questions, multiple contingencies, or probes.

knowledge of the amount and type of information that will be lost.

The second caveat is that extra precautions need to be taken when dealing with certain groups within the population, especially groups that have abnormally large proportions with unusual family patterns. If possible, appropriate steps to cope with this problem should be taken during planning stages of a survey. In the process of questionnaire construction, it may be possible to devise procedures for handling some of the many strange cases that will arise.

The final precaution is against a simple extrapolation of the results of this chapter to reports from other age groups or to reports of other demographic variables. For older respondents the results are probably applicable with little change. This is particularly true for reports of the father's occupation, which is unlikely to be forgotten if it is once learned. Moreover, continued interaction with the father and the "child's" greater awareness of his own and other's occupational roles reinforce his perceptions of the father's job. When the respondents are young children, however, it is likely that the parents' education will be poorly reported (Douvan and Adelson, 1966, p. 318), and even reports of the father's occupation are likely to be less accurate (Coleman et al., 1966, p. 570; Vaillancourt, 1972, p. 50). Other variables such as family income are probably reported very poorly by children of all ages. While many of the findings of the present analysis may be directly applicable to other cohorts and other variables, this cannot be assumed automatically.

These caveats notwithstanding, the results of the present chapter are encouraging. Certainly they will do little to change the procedure for collecting data about family backgrounds, for they essentially tell us to keep doing what we have done in the past, though with added attention to getting details about parental data. They do, however, provide a firm basis for accepting this procedure by indicating that the background information provided by youthful respondents is highly accurate and, therefore, an acceptable substitute for information obtained in a more direct way.

3: Students' Reports of Parents' Political Actions and Attitudes

In this chapter we turn our attention to manifestly political actions and attitudes. Only a few items are available from the student and parent questionnaires, but they cover four distinct and important political phenomena. Two items are directly concerned with voting behavior—whether or not the parent voted in the preceding election, and if so, the partisan direction of the presidential vote. The third piece of information is the parent's party identification or feeling of attachment to one of the political parties.[1] The fourth item taps the parent's level of interest in public affairs and politics. Comparison of the responses from students and their parents for each of these variables will determine the overall accuracy of students' perceptions and will uncover an interesting array of variations in accuracy rates. Substantive implications of the findings will also be discussed.

NATURE OF THE DATA

A fundamental if obvious feature of the variables to be studied here is that both parents and youths are characterized separately on each attribute. Parents and children each have distinguishable partisan attitudes and degrees of political interest. If we are concerned with the early socialization of adults, the "children" as well as their parents have had the opportunity to vote. Otherwise youths can be classified by whether and how they would have voted if they had been eligible.

Although the attributes of parents and youths can be individually

1. Numerous discussions can be found elsewhere of the concept and measurement of party identification and its usefulness in political behavior research. See especially Campbell et al. (1960, chaps. 6–7), Campbell et al. (1966), Almond and Verba (1963, chap. 5).

characterized, it is assumed that there is an intimate, causal connection between the two. The existence of this presumed causal link provides a dual role for youths' perceptions of their parents. On the one hand, youths' reports are often taken as more or less accurate accounts of the parents' positions on a given attribute. This is the usual assumption underlying cross tabulations of the youths' and "perceived-parents' " positions (the latter being reported by the youths). While the exact causal chain from parent to child is commonly left unspecified, these tabulations are interpreted as showing the amount of agreement between youths and their *parents* —and not their parents as perceived by the youths. Similarly, children's reports are sometimes used to show the similarity of husbands' and wives' political characteristics.

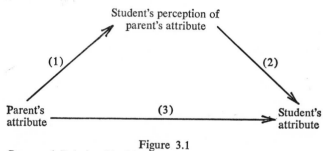

Figure 3.1
Presumed Relationship between Parent and Student Attributes

The second role played by youths' perceptions is that of a link in the causal chain from the parents' to the children's attributes. Although seldom made explicit, it is often assumed that the parental attribute influences the child partly through the latter's perceptions, which may or may not be accurate reflections of the parent's position. Thus, instead of a single parent-child relationship, there is a three-way connection shown in figure 3.1. The major concern is still the total relationship between parent and child attributes, but it is now broken down into a direct component and an indirect component running through the youth's perceptions. As I indicated above, what is usually measured, and called the parent-child relationship, is the link labeled (2). It has often

been observed to be a fairly sizable correlation.[2] The magnitude of
the other two links is only now coming under scrutiny (Jennings
and Niemi, 1968; 1974, chap. 2). We usually assume (1) to be
quite high, and (3) is thought to be very similar to (2), but
there has been no evidence to support either contention.

The reason for pointing out the dual role played by youths' perceptions of their parents is that the analysis below will have implications for both of them. With regard to the first role, one of the
major goals of this chapter is to show how the use of youths' reports as substitutes for parents' reports affects the correlations between parent and child attributes. A consistent but surprisingly
moderate effect will be found. The implications for the second use
of youths' reports are more difficult to specify and would require
an investigation of causal models relating parents' and children's
attributes. My efforts here will be much narrower, being limited
mainly to a descriptive comparison of students' perceptions compared with parents' own reports. While a number of implications
for the whole causal chain will be implicit throughout, no extended
discussion of them will be undertaken.

Concerning the validity of parents' reports, it will generally be
assumed that parents' reports (about themselves but not about
spouses) are correct with regard to voting behavior. Undoubtedly
the risks involved in making this assumption here are greater than
in the case of demographic variables. It has been shown that errors in reporting turnout do occur, and errors in reporting partisan
direction of the vote are also possible.[3] This is especially true
when, as in the present case, respondents are asked to recall their
voting behavior after a lapse of about six months.[4] At the same

2. However, most observations have been made on a very restricted set
of variables, especially party identification. The findings of this chapter, and
direct measurement of the parent-student relationship (Jennings and Niemi,
1968), suggest that for most attributes the correlations expressing (2) are
lower than many observers had thought.

3. A thorough validation study by Clausen (1968–69) confirms that a
small percentage of respondents (a maximum of about 7%) falsely report
whether or not they voted (almost entirely due to nonvoters reporting that
they voted). It casts considerable doubt, however, on the hypothesis that
respondents bias reports of their voting choice by overreporting voting for
the winner.

4. On the positive side, the use of the presidential vote is likely to aid
recall.

time, the fact that the direction of error is known will permit us to specify how it affects the student-parent comparisons.

Errors in reporting party identification and political interest are much harder to identify because the usual procedure for measuring them is to ask respondents, with no independent verification. Even the concept of error is more difficult to pin down. One operational indicator might be the reliability of responses—the extent to which repeated measurements yield the same response (allowing for genuine change). The overall stability of reports of party identification over relatively long periods of time (two and four years) suggests that they are free of gross amounts of error, although responses for very weakly politicized individuals may be unreliable (Campbell et al., 1966, pp. 224–35). There are no comparable data on the stability of responses concerning political interest and, therefore, little basis for determining gross levels of error. We will return to this problem after examining the overall agreement between student and parent reports.

Questions Used in This Study

The questions about voting behavior were straightforward, but care was taken to allow parents to admit gracefully that they had failed to vote. Parents were asked:

> *In talking to people about the presidential election last year between Goldwater and Johnson, we found that a lot of people weren't able to vote because they weren't registered or they were sick or they just didn't have time. How about you, did you vote or did something keep you from voting?* (If voted) *Who did you vote for, for President?*

Students were also asked a two-part question about their parents' vote:

> *Do you happen to know if your father (mother) voted in the presidential election last year between Goldwater and Johnson?* (If yes, voted) *Who did he (she) vote for?*

Students were not asked whether they would have voted if they had been eligible because it was felt that their responses would not be valid indicators anyway. Students' preferences were obtained, however, by asking simply: *If you had been old enough to vote in the election last year between Goldwater and Johnson, who would you have voted for?* (At the time of the study the 18-year-old vote was still several years away.)

Party identification has been determined typically by ascertaining the respondent's subjective affiliation with the party. Here the standard SRC questions were used to obtain the parents' and students' own partisan orientations:

> *Generally speaking, do you usually think of yourself as a Republican, a Democrat, an Independent, or what?* (If Republican or Democrat) *Would you call yourself a strong Republican (Democrat) or a not very strong Republican (Democrat)?* (If Independent) *Do you think of yourself as closer to the Republican or Democratic party?*

Answers from the first question permit us to classify respondents broadly as Democrats, Independents, and Republicans. Use of the follow-up questions yields seven categories along the party identification spectrum. Only a slight modification in wording was required for asking students about their parents. Both initial and follow-up questions were retained.

Political interest of students and parents was tapped by the following question:

> *Some people seem to think about what's going on in government and public affairs most of the time, whether there's an election going on or not. Others aren't that interested. Would you say you follow what's going on in government and public affairs most of the time, some of the time, only now and then, or hardly at all?*

Note that the question asks about attention paid to governmental affairs and not about active participation. Unfortunately, when students were asked about their parents' interest, a slightly different format was used:

> *Would you say your father (mother) is very much interested in public affairs and politics, somewhat interested, or doesn't he (she) pay much attention to it?*

This discrepancy will limit somewhat the usefulness of the political interest item. In particular, no comparison of aggregate student and parent responses will be made, since it is impossible to determine what portion of the difference is due to the question formats. In order to have the same number of response categories for both samples, parents who follow public affairs "only now and then" and "hardly at all" will be combined.

AGGREGATE COMPARISONS

Aggregate student and parent reports of parental voting behavior are given in figure 3.2. The base for the student report of turnout eliminates 5.5 percent of the students who did not know

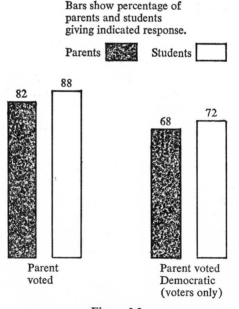

Figure 3.2
Aggregate Student and Parent Reports
of Turnout and Presidential Vote

whether their parent voted. Both student and parent estimates of the Democratic proportion of the vote are based only on voters; also eliminated from the student base is an additional 9 percent of the total sample for whom the direction of the parents' vote was not obtained.

While the estimates for turnout and partisan division of the vote do not differ greatly, the error expected in parents' responses is not only found in students' reports but is present in exaggerated form. Parent reports probably overstate the proportion voting, and yet student reports indicate an even higher turnout. Students also indicate a greater landslide for the Democrats than do the parents.[5] The unwillingness to report nonvoting and the desire to be on the winning side apparently bias youths' responses more than parents', even though the students were reporting parental behavior rather than their own.[6]

An important consequence of the error in student reports is that it affects comparisons of the aggregate parent vote with the overall preferences expressed by the youths. Seventy-four percent of the students said they would have voted for Johnson if they had been old enough. This is only 2 percent more Democratic than the parent vote as estimated by the students but is 6 percent more Democratic than the parent vote as reported by parents themselves. In other words, the generational difference in voting preferences is slightly underestimated by using student reports.

A comparison of student and parent reports of the parent's party identification also reveals small differences. Aggregate reports of the two samples are graphically displayed in figure 3.3. Eliminated from the student base are 7 percent of the students who do not

5. Although the estimates of turnout and the Democratic vote based on the parent sample are high when compared to the national norm, they are very close to estimates based on *comparably aged adults* in the 1964 SRC election study. This suggests that recall error is not a serious problem among the parents. For a discussion of actual turnout figures compared to survey estimates see Clausen (1968–69).

6. It is unlikely that the observed differences are an artifact of using high school seniors, many of whom just completed or were currently enrolled in a civics course. The norm supporting turnout is certainly expressed in civics classes and could account for the overestimate of the proportion voting. But this would leave unaccounted for the greater Democratic vote report by students.

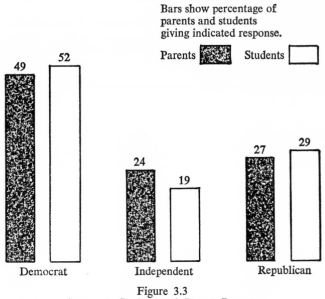

Figure 3.3
Aggregate Student and Parent Reports
of Parent's Party Identification

know their parent's partisan preference. Among the parents, less than 1 percent who are apolitical or minor party identifiers are removed. The chief difference between the two sets of reports is that students slightly underestimate the proportion of Independents in the parent sample. Among the partisans the ratio of Democrats to Republicans among the parents is almost perfectly preserved in the student reports.

In contrast to their reports of the parents' presidential vote, students' reports of party identification exaggerate rather than obscure generational differences. Nearly 36 percent of the students consider themselves Independents, or 12 percent more than among the parents. The difference between students and parents jumps to 17 percent when using youths' perceptions of parental feelings. The tendency for students' reports of party identification to exaggerate generational differences, while their reports of voting behavior obscure them, are contradictory only on the surface. Both results occur because the accuracy of student reports varies within categories of voting behavior and party identification. The basis for these divergent tendencies, which illustrate the difficulty of inferring individual behavior from aggregate results, will be further clarified below, when variations in accuracy rates are considered in detail.

INDIVIDUAL COMPARISONS

Correlations between student and parent reports of political characteristics yield a wide range of values, as indicated in figure 3.4. The correlations are based on student-mother and student-

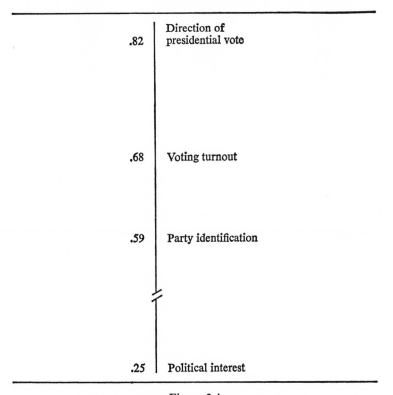

Figure 3.4
Tau-*b* Correlations between Student and Parent
Reports of Parent's Political Characteristics

father pairs combined, but in each case the student's report refers to the particular parent involved in the comparison. For the presidential vote the base is limited to pairs in which both student and parent agreed that the latter voted. The statistic for party identification is based on all seven categories, but there is almost no variation in the correlation when only three or five categories are used.[7]

It is not surprising that students' reports are most accurate regarding voting behavior. Almost everything about the act of voting —that it is highly valued, is likely to be talked about, requires overt action, takes place on a specific day, is the culmination of a period of campaign activity, and so on—helps to make the parent's action or inaction salient for youths. The fact that the question concerned a high stimulus election and the presidential vote makes it even more likely that the parent's voting behavior would be remembered. Somewhat unexpected is the much higher correlation for the direction of the vote than for turnout. Since it is the voting act that is public, we might hypothesize that turnout would be reported more accurately than partisan choice. Analysis below will indicate that the reversal is due to the fact that students often do not know or are unwilling to admit that their parents did not vote. When the parent did vote, students report this fact as accurately as the partisan choice.

Evaluation of the correlation for party identification depends, even more than the others, on one's initial expectations. It is so often tacitly assumed that partisan attitudes are reported "very

7. For turnout it is possible to obtain a good estimate of the effects of nonstudent error. Assume that 7% of the parents erroneously reported that they had voted (see n. 4). Next, suppose that the proportion of students who correctly reported their parents' behavior was the same for parents who correctly reported not voting and for the 7% who erroneously reported voting. Recalculating the correlation on the basis of these "adjusted" data yields $\tau_b = .71$. This figure can be evaluated against the correlation between student and parent reports of the number of children in the family (using only families in which both natural parents are present). This seems like a reasonable way to correct for interviewer, coder, and keypuncher errors. Thus $.71/.96 = .74$. The difference between this figure and 1.0 can probably be attributed entirely to student error.

For direction of the presidential vote, the effects of parental error are probably even smaller than for turnout (see n. 4). For party identification the effects are probably somewhat larger, but we have no way of making a precise estimate. The possibility of unreliability of responses to the political interest item is commented or in the text.

accurately" that it is sobering to realize that the reports are far from perfect. Some students do misperceive their parent's party affiliation, occasionally by a great deal. Thus there remains a definite possibility, to be examined below, that the use of student rather than parent reports significantly affects our understanding of the parent-student relationship. At the same time, a correlation of .59 does indicate a relatively high degree of accuracy among student reports. This is especially true when it is considered that partisan commitment is attitudinal rather than factual in nature. That reports of an attitudinal variable even approach the level of accuracy obtained for factual data is abundant evidence of the salience of that attitude. Certainly few, if any, other political attitudes of parents are perceived this accurately by youths.

The weight of these considerations is forcefully conveyed by the low correlation for political interest.[8] Agreement between student and parent reports of the latter's interest is no higher than for some of the items concerning family structure and relationships (see chapter 5). Two possible explanations can be suggested for the low correlation. A straightforward interpretation is that students do in fact perceive parental political interest very inaccurately. In contrast to active participation, interest in politics can be a relatively private affair, carried on, for example, by close attention to one or more of the mass media. To the extent that individuals engage in overt actions, such as political discussions, they need not be carried out in the home; even if they are, they may go unnoticed by youths. Moreover, to some extent the level of interest is a matter of personal feeling apart from one's behavior. While

8. It may be necessary to allay the suspicion that the low correlation is an artifact of using different formats for the student and parent questions. Logically this could happen, for it is known that the marginal distributions of two variables can greatly restrict their degree of association when cross-tabulated (Blalock, 1960, pp. 231–32, 323). In this particular case, with the marginals obtained for the student and parent samples, the maximum tau-b is .71. Even if evaluated against this maximum ($.25/.71 = .35$), the correlation for political interest is well below those for the other political variables (the values of which are also slightly restricted by different student and parent marginals). Additional support for the validity of this correlation is found in the Hess and Torney "sibling" study. They included one item on parents' political interest. The product-moment correlation between siblings' reports of their parents' political interest (.13) is even lower than that observed here. See Hess and Torney (1965, p. 441).

children may closely monitor their parents' behavior, they are much less likely to know parents' feelings.

A second possible explanation for the low correlation is that in many cases parents' reports of political interest do not represent stable, enduring orientations to the political world. Responses to the political interest question may be very unstable over time, fluctuating in nearly random fashion. This was the pattern found by Converse (1964) for attitudes toward a number of political issues during the late 1950s. Using panel data from the American electorate, Converse demonstrated that professed attitudes on some of the major contemporary controversies varied over two- and four-year intervals in such a way that they could just as well have been generated randomly for many respondents. Instability of opinions was a result of the lack of centrality of political issues for most individuals, among other things. While they responded to survey items, respondents' answers did not reflect the pervasive, orderly attitude structure that was found at that time among political elites. If response to the political interest item were also unstable for many parents, it is hardly surprising that students' reports are of limited accuracy, inasmuch as they are trying to report a fluctuating characteristic.

Although students were not asked about their parents' attitudes on other political issues, the accuracy of their perceptions probably would have been of the same magnitude as for political interest, rather than for party identification. This follows from the findings of the study just cited, in which Converse discussed the structure of political attitudes among mass publics. Given the nearly random nature of many individuals' responses to policy questions, we can be virtually certain that large numbers of students could not accurately identify the responses given by their parents. In contrast to attitudes on specific policies, we noted earlier that partisan attitudes were highly stable over two- and four-year periods, reflecting a rather basic orientation to the party system.[9] Hence, for party identification the accuracy of student

9. The greater issue awareness of the 1960s compared to the 1950s (see, for example, Pomper, 1972) suggests that the accuracy of youths' views of parents will also vary across time. Most often, however, we would expect these perceptions to be less accurate than for partisanship.

reports is much less affected by the instability of parental reports and is consequently of a much greater magnitude.

Accuracy of Student Reports within Categories of Voting Behavior and Party Identification

To judge properly student reports of parent political characteristics, we need to know more than the overall rates of accuracy, as summarized by the correlations given above. In particular, it is important to know whether the accuracy of student reports depends on the exact categorization of the parent. In this section, student reports of parental voting behavior and party loyalty are analyzed with this in mind. Political interest must again be excluded, because the accuracy rates within categories of interest are related to the marginal distributions and so are largely determined by the use of different student and parent questions.

Students' reports of the parents' turnout for the November 1964 election could hardly have been more accurate in terms of percentage agreement. The reports of 92 percent of the students agreed with reports given by their parents. An interesting difference appears, however, when separate percentages are calculated for voters and nonvoters. As shown in table 3.1, students and

Table 3.1
Percentage of Students Accurately
Reporting Parent's Voting Behavior

Student's Report	Parent's Report	
	Voted	*Did not vote*
Voted	98	39
Did not vote	2	61
N	1,456	274

parents almost unanimously agreed when parents said they had voted. But when the parent failed to vote, only about 60 percent of the students accurately reported this. The much lower rate of accuracy in the nonvoter category accounts for the slight overestimate of turnout observed in students' reports. It is also the reason that the student-parent correlation is lower than might be expected from the extremely high percentage agreement.

A similar but much smaller difference is found in students' reports of the candidate for whom the parent voted. Of the pairs in which both student and parent indicated the presidential vote, slightly over 92 percent agreed on the candidate supported. However, the students reported votes for Johnson more faithfully than they reported Goldwater votes (table 3.2). The difference is not

Table 3.2
Percentage of Students Accurately
Reporting Parent's Presidential Vote

Student's Report	Parent's Report	
	Johnson	Goldwater
Johnson	96	16
Goldwater	4	84
N	882	384

as striking as in the case of turnout, so it leads to a smaller overestimate of the Johnson vote and has a less depressing effect on the student-parent correlation.[10]

It was noted in connection with the aggregate comparisons that bias in student reports could account for the overestimates of turnout and of the Democratic proportion of the vote. The contribution of bias to the individual patterns can simply be noted here. Bias in student accounts will almost always take the form of reports that the parent voted when he did not or that he voted for Johnson when he actually cast a ballot for Goldwater. If the parent reports his behavior correctly, the effect of these errors is to lower

10. I have pointed out that the variations in the accuracy of student reports within categories of voting behavior explain the slight differences in aggregate student and parent reports. It should be noted, however, that these same variations could result in gross errors in aggregate student reports under some rather ordinary circumstances. A simple example demonstrates this. Suppose the actual parental turnout for an election had been 50%. If we use the accuracy rates found above, students would have reported the turnout as $.50 \times .98 + .50 \times .39 = .685$ or 68.5%! I am not suggesting that such large errors usually or even very often occur. However, the example does illustrate one type of potential problem created when accuracy rates depend on the precise categorization of the parent.

the accuracy rate among nonvoters and among Goldwater supporters. Note, however, that if the parent also misrepresents his behavior on the side of turnout or voting for Johnson, the student reports will appear to be accurate. Thus, some of the cases in which the student and parent reports agree that the parent went to the polls or that he voted for Johnson are a result of bias in both sets of reports. Only when the parent erred but the student accurately reported his behavior (plus the small number of cases in which student bias is toward nonvoting or toward Goldwater support) will errors be noted in the "voted" or "voted for Johnson" columns.

The accuracy of student reports of parental party identification varies greatly with the partisanship of the parent.[11] A tabular comparison of the two reports is given in table 3.3; for convenience the

Table 3.3
Student and Parent Reports of Parent's Party Identification
(In percentages)

Student's Report	Parent's Report						
	Strong Dem.	*Weak Dem.*	*Ind. Dem.*	*Ind.*	*Ind. Rep.*	*Weak Rep.*	*Strong Rep.*
Democrat	89	71	53	33	17	14	8
Independent	8	18	37	51	37	13	9
Republican	3	11	10	16	46	73	84
Total	100	100	100	100	100	100	101
N	414	416	146	149	83	251	205

student responses have been collapsed into the three major categories. It is immediately apparent that partisan commitments are most accurately perceived when they are strongly held. Over 87 percent of the strong partisans are correctly identified by their children, and less than 5 percent are perceived to identify with the

11. The proportion of students who do not know their parent's party identification is also related to strength of partisanship, as follows:

	Parent Report						
	Strong Dem.	*Weak Dem.*	*Ind. Dem.*	*Ind.*	*Ind. Rep.*	*Weak Rep.*	*Strong Rep.*
% of students DK	5	6	14	14	7	6	3

opposite party. As one moves toward the middle of the partisan dimension, reports become much less accurate. Whether the decreasing accuracy is monotonic, however, is partly a matter of interpretation. Using the traditional cutting points of Democrat, Independent, and Republican (i.e., using the responses to the initial question but not the follow-up), we find that students' perceptions are poorest among parents who are basically Independent but lean toward one of the parties. Among Independent Democrats and Independent Republicans, only 37 percent of the students correctly indicated that the parent was basically Independent. This is well below the 51 percent who accurately perceived the parent's basic orientation when the parent did not lean toward either party. On the other hand, the deviations in the students' reports of Independent Democrats and Republicans are not evenly distributed but heavily favor the party to which the parent feels closer. Even though the basically Independent outlook of the parents is often not perceived, their partisan inclinations are usually recognized.[12]

Studies of voting and other kinds of political participation suggest several reasons why students' reports become more accurate as the intensity of the parents' partisanship increases. Most important is that increased partisanship is associated with greater interest in politics (Milbrath, 1965, p. 53; Verba and Nie, 1972, chap. 12). Strong identifiers pay more attention to public affairs and are more concerned with the flow of political events. They more often participate in public affairs, especially partisan activities. For these reasons, intense partisans undoubtedly emit stronger and more frequent cues, which enable children to classify them properly. Conversely, the weaker the parents' party loyalties, the

12. Instead of utilizing the traditional cutting points, we might consider student reports as reasonably accurate if they coincide perfectly with the parents' self-placement on the sevenfold identification spectrum or if they are within one category on either side of the parents' report. Interpreted in this way, the following percentages of students give accurate reports:

	Parent Report						
	Strong Dem.	Weak Dem.	Ind. Dem.	Ind.	Ind. Rep.	Weak Rep.	Strong Rep.
% of students accurate	89	80	63	51	59	78	84

less likely they are to convey their feelings in their words and actions. Consequently, youths must rely on fewer and more ambiguous signals to classify their parents, with more errors as a result.

It may also be more difficult to transmit an Independent orientation unless it is consciously and deliberately conveyed. Undoubtedly most Independents emit cues which, taken out of context, are partisan in nature. Unless these cues are delicately balanced between the parties—and are perceived as such—the parents will be reported as partisans. In addition, some youths may determine their parents' loyalty on the basis of their voting behavior, focusing mainly on a few major contests. If an Independent parent happens to favor the major candidates of one party for successive elections, he may be reported as identifying with that party. These explanations suggest why the partisan inclination of Independent Democrats and Republicans is accurately perceived while their basically Independent stance is overlooked. Independent leaners are more likely than nonleaners to support one party's candidates regularly, and their evaluations of political affairs are more likely to be consistently in one direction. Apparently, in many cases youths focus on these relatively consistent partisan cues and ignore or simply fail to notice the Independent outlook that the parent professes.

Strength of partisanship accounts for the major variation observed in table 3.3. Note, however, that the accuracy rates are not perfectly symmetric. Students' reports are more accurate for strong Democratic than for strong Republican parents and for Independent Democrats than for Independent Republicans. (Accuracy rates are about the same for weak partisans of both parties.) At least two factors contribute to these differences. First of all, there may be a slight tendency for students to see parents as supporting the dominant party, in the same way that they overreport voting for the winning presidential candidate. For this reason some children of Republican parents may alter their perceptions in the Democratic direction. Secondly, since many more students personally identify with the Democrats than with the Republicans, bias toward the students' own preferences results in less accuracy among children of Republicans. These same two factors also contribute to the fact that children of Independents see their parents as Democrats much more often than as Republicans.

Self-directed Bias in Students' Reports

Potentially the most significant type of error in students' reports is bias in the direction of the students' own values and preferences. Such bias may serve an important psychological function for youths, by making it appear to themselves and others that they are not really so different from their parents, but it seriously threatens the use of youths' reports as accurate indicators of parental attributes. To the extent that youths' reports are reflections of their own feelings, the operation of matching children's attributes with parental attributes as reported by children is circular. Attributes of the two generations will appear to be congruent simply because that is the way youths see them.

The observed accuracy rates of student reports are high enough to dismiss the most extreme possibility—that the students' attributes correlate highly with their own reports of parental characteristics but correlate very poorly or even negatively with the parents' true features. At the same time, misperceptions were frequent enough that the use of students' reports could overestimate the congruity of student and parent attributes. The likelihood of an overestimate, as well as its magnitude, depends on the amount of self-directed bias in the student reports.

The amount of bias will be judged by the proportion of students whose report of the parent's attribute differs from that parent's report and is closer to the student's own attribute. This measure is described in the appendix with an example from chapter 5. It is somewhat ironic that self-directed bias is greatest for the variable most accurately reported. Although over 90 percent of the students correctly reported their parent's vote, 69 percent of the incorrect reports are in the direction of the student's own preference. For both party identification and political interest, 61 percent of the erroneous reports are in the direction of the student's own attribute.[13]

13. Turnout will not be treated here because students were not classified by whether or not they would have voted.

An interpretation of these amounts of bias is best made by observing their effect on the apparent relationship between student and parent attributes. This is provided in figure 3.5 for all three

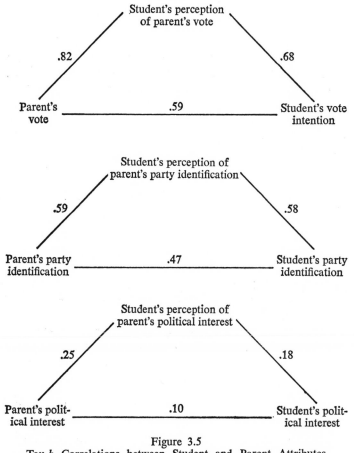

Figure 3.5
Tau-*b* Correlations between Student and Parent Attributes
Using Students' Perceptions of Parents and Parents' Own Reports

variables. The correlations between parent attributes and student perceptions of them (upper-left diagonal) are repeated here for convenience. The correlations between the parent and student attributes are given on the lower line in each triangle, while the correlations between the student attributes and the student report of the parent attributes are given on the upper-right diagonal. As a result of self-directed bias, the use of student reports overestimates the actual student-parent correlation by an average of almost .10.[14] The effect is consistent despite the wide variations in the accuracy of student perceptions and in the degree of student-parent congruity.

The magnitude and consistency of the effects due to self-directed bias are both surprising and encouraging. Considering the extreme hypothetical examples that can be constructed, the degree to which the student-parent correlations were overestimated by using student reports is rather small. Moreover, the consistency of the overestimate for all three attributes suggests that the effect on other political variables may be of the same magnitude.

To be sure, the size of the overestimate varies within control categories. This would be expected on the basis of sampling variability alone. To gain some purchase on these variations, five different controls (family politicization, parent-student sex combinations, region, parent's education, and student political interest —except when interest itself was considered) were applied to each of the three attributes, making a total of fifty-seven control categories. The overestimates formed a reasonably symmetric distribution with a mean of .10. In addition, the means for the categories of each control variable for each attribute separately were all in the range .10 ± .03. As expected, a few extreme values were found. The overestimates ranged as high as .26 in one instance and as low as −.02 in another (the only underestimate that occurred).[15] Thus while the overestimate will occasionally be very

14. It must be remembered that the numerical value of the overestimate depends on the statistic used. For example, the γ correlation suggested by Goodman and Kruskal (1954, p. 749) yields differences of about .14 for two of the items. For the presidential vote, the γ correlation using the parents' own reports is so high that a ceiling effect is imposed, and the overestimate is only .04.

15. The distribution of the overestimates of the student-parent correlations was as follows:

Amount of overestimate	≤.04	.05–.07	.08–.12	.13–.15	≥.16
Number of control categories	6 (11%)	15 (26%)	20 (35%)	8 (14%)	8 (14%)

small or quite large, one can expect it to be in the range of .05–.15 most of the time.[16]

This does not mean that an unwanted inflation of about .05–.15 in the size of student–"perceived-parent" correlations should be ignored. Undoubtedly this is one factor that contributed to the view that youths' political values are more highly congruent with their parents' values than has lately been found (Jennings and Niemi, 1968). The results do suggest, however, that simple corrections can be made for the effect of self-directed bias on the estimated correlation between student and parent political characteristics. This means that studies relying on a single sample can be expected to yield reasonably valid approximations of the actual correlation between student and parent attributes.

Correlates of Accurate Student Reports

On a superficial level the search for correlates of accurate student reports proved notably unsuccessful. Although variations in accuracy rates were found, they sometimes ran contrary to hypothesized directions. In other cases the rates of accuracy within control groups were really indeterminant due to small numbers of cases in certain cells (e.g., Goldwater voters among blacks). Most important, when certain control groups did reveal systematic differences in accuracy rates for one variable, similar differences were not observed in the reports of other variables. Another level of analysis, however, uncovered variations in accuracy rates that shed considerable light on the processes underlying student responses. At times these variations involve correlates in the usual sense of the term; students with certain characteristics respond more accurately than others to questions about their parents. In other cases the variations in accuracy are a result of a more complex pattern

16. There are exceptions, of course, when the distributions within control categories are pathological. Among blacks, for example, the overestimate of the student-parent correlation for party identification is, not surprisingly, quite high (.23) because the distribution is highly skewed in the Democratic direction. However, it is also true that in several cases a relationship that emerged using parents' reports was covered up by the use of students' reports. For an example and the substantive interpretation, see Jennings and Niemi (1974, chap. 2).

of interaction between the parental attribute and other characteristics of the parents.

Particularly striking is the difference between voting turnout and political interest on the one hand and party identification and partisan direction of the vote on the other. In contrast to the latter pair, reports of turnout and interest are unrelated to several variables that seem likely to affect student accuracy. Instead, they reveal patterns that suggest that some students responded in terms of their expectations about their parents or about parents in general. Another term for this phenomenon is "educated guessing." When students were not positive about their parents' attitudes or behavior, some of them probably reasoned that their parents "must have" felt or behaved a certain way. Such inferences might be based on the parents' past behavior or on what students expect of them.

One example is provided by differences in the accuracy of reporting turnout among fathers and mothers. When the father or mother voted, students were highly accurate in reports about either sex—99 and 97 percent of the time for fathers and mothers, respectively. But when the parent reported that he or she failed to vote, students accurately noted this for only 47 percent of the fathers in contrast to 65 percent of the mothers. The greater accuracy of reporting nonvoting among mothers, and the barely noticeable differences between mothers and fathers who voted, are what one would expect if some students "guessed" about their parent's behavior. Since men are expected to take a more active part in politics than women, students who are unsure about their parent's behavior will more often say that their fathers voted than their mothers. This means that when the parents actually voted, students who "guess" will more often be correct about their fathers; conversely when the parents failed to vote, they will more frequently be right about their mothers.[17] Now suppose these students

17. This might be illustrated with arbitrary figures (given in percentages) as follows:

Students' Report	Parent voted		Parent did not vote	
	Fathers	*Mothers*	*Fathers*	*Mothers*
Voted	*70*	*60*	*70*	*60*
Did not vote	30	40	*30*	*40*

are added to those who did not guess about their parents. The addition will have little effect on the accuracy rates for parents who voted because this is such a large number of cases. If it does make a detectable difference, it will tend to increase the rate of accuracy for fathers compared to mothers. There is a much smaller number of nonvoters, however, so the addition of those who "guessed" will have a greater effect on accuracy rates. It will tend to make reports of mothers more accurate than reports of fathers.[18]

A second example suggesting that some students respond in terms of their expectations is provided by the different levels of accuracy in reporting turnout among blacks compared to whites. Ninety-eight percent of the white students and 96 percent of the blacks accurately reported their parent's behavior when the parent voted. Among nonvoters, however, 57 percent of the white students but 91 percent of the blacks correctly indicated the failure to go to the polls. Like the difference in reporting turnout of fathers and mothers, the greater accuracy in reporting nonvoting among blacks may be partially due to a guessing factor. If black students were unsure about their parents' behavior, they would probably report nonvoting more frequently than whites.

A difference in subcultural norms may also contribute heavily to the variations in accuracy between whites and blacks. White students undoubtedly expect their parents to vote in large proportions. It may be hard for them to admit to themselves or to others that their parents failed to perform their "citizen duty." Over-reporting of voting is a direct result. Among blacks the voting norm is certainly less thoroughly ingrained, partly because they have often been prevented from casting their ballots in the past. Nonvoting is therefore more acceptable behavior, and there is little psychological pressure on black youth to falsify their reports of nonvoting parents.[19]

The correct student reports are shown in italics. Students "guessed" that 70% of the fathers and 60% of the mothers voted. As indicated in the text, among voters (nonvoters) students are more often right about fathers (mothers).

18. "Guessing" probably does not account for the entire difference between the accuracy rates for men and women. Youths may be more willing to admit that their mother failed to vote than their father.

19. Voting direction among blacks cannot be treated because there was exactly one black parent who said he voted for Goldwater.

Other indications that responses were sometimes made on the basis of students' expectations were also found. For example, it was originally hypothesized that student reports of parents' political characteristics would be more accurate among highly politicized families. In the case of turnout, the data lend no support to the hypothesis. Among parents who voted, there are practically no variations at all in the rate of student accuracy. Even in the least politicized families, 95 percent of the students correctly indicated that the parent voted.[20] Sizable variations do occur in reporting nonvoting but, surprisingly, the lowest rates of accuracy are among the most politicized families! Students' strong expectations that their parents will vote, or a greater sensitivity about reporting nonvoting, apparently overshadow any perceptual gain from the highly politicized environment.

Students' reports of the parents' political interest also show indications that responses were sometimes made on the basis of students' expectations. Earlier it was noted that variations in the accuracy of student reports within categories of interest were due largely to the distribution of parent and student responses, which were in turn affected by the use of different student and parent questions. For example, the fact that 41 percent of the parents who say they are very interested are also rated by their children as highly interested has little intrinsic meaning. While this is true, there is no reason to expect the question formats to affect the variations in student accuracy rates differentially within control groups. In the example just given, there is no reason to expect that the accuracy rates among highly interested men or women, say, should differ from 41 percent by more than sampling error. And yet this is precisely what happens. For parents in the highest interest category, student reports are accurate 46 percent of the time for fathers and only 34 percent of the time for mothers. In the middle category, the accuracy rates are similar for both sexes, but in the lowest category of interest the rates again differ. This time the accuracy rate for mothers (26 percent) is higher than that for fathers (16 percent). As with reports of voting turnout, the differences by sex of the parent coincide with expectations about men's and women's political interest.

20. The measure of politicization is defined below (see table 3.5).

Another example of varying rates of accuracy in reports of political interest shows even more strikingly the effects of responses based on expectations. In table 3.4, parents are grouped by their education and by their own reports of political interest. The percentage in each cell shows the proportion of students correctly identifying their parent's level of interest. Among parents with only a grade school education, students' reports are equally accurate for the highly interested and the rather uninterested. As education increases, the reports of highly interested parents become progressively more accurate, and reports of uninterested parents become steadily less so. Some students apparently assume that highly edu-

Table 3.4
Percentage of Students Correctly Identifying Parent's Political Interest,
by Parent's Level of Interest and Education

Parent's Political Interest (own report)	Parent's Education (own report)							
	Grade school		*High school*		*College*		*Graduate education*	
	%	N	%	N	%	N	%	N
High	32	158	34	608	52	322	71	61
Medium	64	156	68	427	68	115	*	
Low	33	179	19	259	14	26	*	

* Less than 10 cases.

cated parents are interested in politics and so judge them; it is more befitting less-educated parents to be uninterested in public affairs, and consequently more are reported to lack interest. When parents' own reports coincide with these expectations, students' reports are correct. When they conflict with student expectations, however, students have "guessed" wrong.

Reports of the parents' party identifications do not entirely escape the problem of responses in terms of expectations. When reports of party loyalty are observed separately for blacks and whites, it appears that black students are much more accurate reporters of Democratic parents and much less accurate reporters of non-Democratic parents. For example, among both strong and weak Democrats, 95 percent of the black students correctly indicated their parent's party preference; the corresponding figures for whites are 89 percent among strong Democrats and 69 percent for weak Democrats. There are so few black Independents (N = 20) and Republicans (N = 13) that they must be lumped together to get a sufficient number of cases. When this is done, only 21 percent of the black students correctly identified the parent's partisan attitude. This is far below the accuracy rate for any category of white parents. Significantly, 73 percent of the black students with non-Democratic parents reported them as Democratic anyway. Obviously most black youths expected their parents to be Democratic and were largely unaware of it when the parent expressed any other sentiment.[21]

Despite the example just discussed, student reports of the parents' party identification and presidential vote seem much less affected by the problem of response expectations. In part this means that certain variations observed in reports of turnout and political interest were not found in reports of party loyalty and the vote. For example, the correlations between student and parent reports of party identification were almost the same for fathers (.60) and mothers (.58). The same is true for presidential voting, where the correlations were .83 for fathers and .81 for mothers. On the other hand, reports of partisanship and voting also vary systematically where the other variables showed inconsistent movement. Family politicization, for example, is highly related to accuracy rates, as is shown by the correlations in table 3.5. For both variables there is a monotonic and rather sharp decrease in the level of student accuracy as the degree of politicization is lowered.

Turning briefly to one other control variable, we find no major differences in the accuracy of student reports of party identification within regions of the country. The correlations are as follows: Northeast .57, Midwest .62, South .56 (whites only, .58), West .61. Accuracy rates within party identification categories by region show mostly minor variations, but two points are worth noting.

21. The findings reported in this paragraph are partly due to self-directed bias. That is, bias in the direction of black youths' own attitudes almost always takes the form of reporting Independent and Republican parents as Democrats. However, even black students who consider themselves Independent and Republican most often see their parents as Democrats. In the extreme case of 13 non-Democratic students whose parents also consider themselves non-Democratic, 7 (54%) report them as Democrats anyway.

Table 3.5
Tau-*b* Correlations between Student and Parent Reports of
Parent's Voting Behavior and Party Identification,
by Level of Politicization

Variable	Level of Politicization[a]					
	High					*Low*
	1	2	3	4	5	6
Direction of presidential vote	.91	.82	.82	.80	.73	.71
N	142	239	277	233	140	83
Party identification	.64	.62	.60	.58	.51	.47
N	173	292	365	309	197	128

[a] This is an index combining parents' reports of husband-wife political conversations and students' reports of student-parent political discussions. The construction is similar to that described in chap. 2, n. 14.

First, there is no greater accuracy among white children of Southern Democrats than among Democrats as a whole. Nor is there less accuracy among white children of Southern Republicans than among all Republicans. Moreover, when reporting errors are made by Southern whites, there is no tendency to report parents as Democratic to a greater extent than is observed in other regions. Unlike blacks, Southern whites do not assume that their parents are necessarily Democratic. The other important point is that children of Republicans in the West give accurate reports somewhat more often than those in other regions. Perhaps a greater proportion of extreme conservatives among Western Republicans makes their party affiliations more obvious than usual.

HUSBAND-WIFE SIMILARITY

The homogeneity or heterogeneity of the family environment plays an important role in the political socialization of youth. For one thing, the amount of mother-father agreement directly affects the transmission of values from parent to child by determining the extent to which uniform or competing stimuli come from the parents. Secondly, parental similarity indirectly affects the transmission process since agreement or disagreement contributes to the amount and style of husband-wife interaction regarding politics and public affairs. A third way in which parental similarity may alter the flow of values between generations is by affecting youths' perceptions of their parents. A common assumption is that youths' perceptions are more accurate when parents hold congruent political views or share common political orientations. If this is true, it probably tends to increase the similarity of attributes between homogeneous parents and their children (assuming that youths generally do not rebel).

In this section, three interrelated issues will be considered. Initially it is asked whether the students' perceptions of one parent are biased toward the perceived attributes of the other parent (when the parents are viewed as dissimilar). Assuming that such bias exists, we consider the possibility that student reports make the husband and wife appear more similar than they are according to their own reports. Finally, a direct comparison will be made of the accuracy of student reports when the husband and wife are similar and when they are dissimilar.

Bias toward the Perceived Attribute of the Other Parent

Students' reports of all four political variables reveal a substantial bias toward the perceived attribute of the other parent. Using the measure of bias described in the appendix, we find that political interest and party identification show about the same amount of distortion, with 70 percent and 71 percent, respectively, of the erroneous reports being closer to the perceived interest or partisan loyalty of the second parent. Reports of turnout and the presidential vote are biased to a greater extent. Eighty-four percent of the incorrect reports of turnout and 79 percent of those for the direction of the vote match the perceived behavior of the other parent.

Since this bias is toward the *perceived* attribute of the second parent, its presence does not guarantee that husband and wife will appear more similar in student reports than in parents' own reports. Nevertheless, the large amounts of bias observed, coupled with the fairly high overall accuracy rates (except for political interest), strongly suggests that students do in fact see parents as more similar than they really are. Using the 430 families in which both parents were interviewed, we can calculate the correlations between the husbands' and wives' attributes from both parent and student reports. The results, given in table 3.6, show that student reports consistently overestimate the amount of agreement between husband and wife. The magnitude of the overestimate is greatest for political interest, which is the variable reported least accurately by the students. At the other extreme, there is a ceiling effect operating on reports of the presidential vote. Students perceive the parents' votes so accurately, and husbands and wives so often vote for the same candidate anyway, that there is only a trace of increased parental similarity using student reports.

Table 3.6
Similarity of Husband and Wife
Using One versus Two Sources of Information

Topic	Source of Information about		Tau-*b* Correlations between Characteristics of Husband and Wife[a]
	Husband	*Wife*	
Party	Husband	Wife	.60
identification	Student	Student	.66
Political	Husband	Wife	.27
interest	Student	Student	.38
Turnout	Husband	Wife	.44
	Student	Student	.52
Presidential	Husband	Wife	.82
vote	Student	Student	.83

[a] These correlations are based on the 430 families in which both parents were interviewed.

The consistent overestimate of parental similarity is apparently part of a general tendency to overestimate similarity when using only one of two or more independent sources of information. This will become clearer in chapter 5 where we will find the same tendency operating in reports of family and parental characteristics.

Accuracy of Perceptions for Similar and Dissimilar Parents

A likely correlate of bias toward the perceived attribute of the other parent is that students' perceptions are more accurate when husband and wife are similar rather than dissimilar. If parents hold common views or behave identically, their shared attribute probably reinforces the students' perception of each of them. Competing views or opposing behaviors offer conflicting stimuli that may distract from the students' perception of both parents. Moreover, if we assume that the attribute of one parent is quite accurately perceived and that the perception of the other parent is biased toward the view of the first, reporting errors will result only when the parents differ. (Another way of saying this is that there is really no measurable bias when the parents are similar.) Undoubtedly there are some families for which a contrasting line of reasoning is appropriate. Dissimilarity sometimes offers a sharp contrast that makes each parent's attribute more salient. Admitting that this occasionally happens, we hypothesize that parental similarity will lead to accurate student views much more often than dissimilarity.

The data generally support the hypothesis, but there are some interesting variations among the four variables. Reports of turnout and the presidential vote show substantially different rates of accuracy for homogeneous and heterogeneous parents (table 3.7). For

Table 3.7
Student and Parent Reports of Turnout and Direction of
Presidential Vote, among Homogeneous and Heterogeneous Parents
(In percentages)

Student's Report	Parent's Report			
	Homogeneous parents[a]		*Heterogeneous parents*[a]	
	Voted	Did not vote	*Voted*	Did not vote
Voted	99	38	95	61
Did not vote	1	62	5	39
N	736	53	73	69
	$\tau_b = .69$		$\tau_b = .41$	
	Johnson	*Goldwater*	*Johnson*	*Goldwater*
Johnson	93	11	83	44
Goldwater	2	89	17	56
N	370	209	23	25
	$\tau_b = .88$		$\tau_b = .40$	

NOTE: The top and bottom halves of this table are each based on the 430 families in which the student, mother, and father were interviewed. However, the NS give the combined number of student-mother and student-father pairs, for which the unweighted N = 860 (weighted N = 1,062).
[a] Among homogeneous parents, husband and wife acted identically (e.g., both voted); among heterogeneous parents, husband and wife acted differently.

both variables the reports are more accurate when the parents behaved identically. The differences are especially large for the behavior reported less accurately overall. It was shown earlier that students report voting by their parents more accurately than non-voting. Here it can be added that students accurately report that one parent voted even if the other did not. Among nonvoters, however, reports are much more accurate (although still far less so than for voters) when both parents failed to vote. Similarly, reports of Goldwater votes are particularly inaccurate when the other parent voted for Johnson.

The effects of parental similarity weighed somewhat less heavily on student reports of party identification and political interest. By cross-tabulating the husbands' and wives' placement on the seven-category party identification ranking, parents were divided into three groups: the first group contains pairs in which the husband's and wife's placement matched perfectly; the second group includes those differing by only a single category, while the last group consists of the remaining pairs. As expected, student reports are most accurate when the parents agree completely ($\tau_b = .67$). However, reports of husbands and wives who disagree only slightly are barely less accurate (.64). It is only when parents show moderate to strong disagreement that reports become less reliable (.40).[22] Student reports of parental political interest are somewhat more accurate when parents have similar rather than contrasting levels of interest (.25 versus .16). The difference is not large, however, and is due mainly to more accurate reports of one highly interested parent when the other parent is also very interested.

At the beginning of this chapter, a distinction was made between two major roles played by youths' reports of their parents' political characteristics. On the one hand, they are considered very accurate substitutes for the parents' own reports. As such they are

22. The distribution of parents along the party identification spectrum is fairly uniform for parents who agree or who disagree only slightly, but there are more Independents in the third group of parents. This by itself lowers the correlation between student and parent reports since Independent parents are less accurately reported. However, inspection of the percentages within each category of party loyalty shows that students' perceptions definitely suffer when parents have moderate to strong disagreements.

used chiefly to indicate the amount of agreement between parents and youths, presumably indicating the impact of one generation on the next. On the other hand, it is sometimes acknowledged that youths' reports are indeed perceptions, which are subject to various sorts of errors and biases. In this role, youths' perceptions are posited as an explicit link in the causal chain from parents' to youths' attributes.

The implications of the current findings are moderately favorable with regard to the first of these roles. Youths' reports are not, however, completely accurate substitutes for parents' own accounts. The data reveal only one variable reported with about the same overall accuracy as the parents' education and occupation (which is perhaps a better comparison than hypothetical perfect reports). Perceptions of two other items were also quite accurate on the whole. The remaining attribute, political interest, was reported very inaccurately, and I suggested that this is probably typical of many other political attitudes. Most importantly, there were hints (see note 10 above) that the similarity of aggregate reports is artifactual, depending on the distribution of voters versus nonvoters and partisans versus Independents. This important matter will be returned to in chapter 4 and again in chapter 7.

Nevertheless, when student reports are used to estimate the student-parent relationship—and this is probably the major use of children's reports—a consistent and moderate bias is found; correlations between student and perceived parent attributes overestimated the actual student-parent correlations by about .10 for each of three variables. Similarly student reports overestimated the congruency between husbands and wives, but only moderately so. While it would be desirable to confirm these findings for a wider range of political attributes, the consistency of the results suggests that simple corrections can be made to counteract the effects of self-directed bias in youths' reports.

The implications of reporting errors (or perhaps "perceptual errors" is a better term) for the other major role played by youths' reports are of an entirely different order and will require a separate, extensive analysis. In this role, youths' perceptions of their parents are viewed as one of the major contributors to their own attitudes and behavior. Whether and to what extent these perceptions are accurate is a key *variable,* and perceptions are in no sense required to be highly accurate or even moderately correct. Here I have documented the overall accuracy rates for students' perceptions of several political attributes and have outlined some of the variations in rates of accuracy as they depend on the specific categorization of the parent and on characteristics of the family and child.

A number of the findings are especially relevant for understanding the role of perceptions in the flow of attitudes and values from parents to youths. In addition to the wide range of overall accuracy, variations were found within categories of each attribute. It was also found that when the parental attitude was more strongly held, as in the case of strong party identifiers, perceptions tended to be more accurate. On the other hand, student perceptions were somewhat misguided when parental attributes failed to match student expectations, suggesting that youths fail to absorb information that is contrary to their general impression of their parents. Finally, similarity between husband and wife made student perceptions more accurate.

These findings give some idea of the complex part played by youths' perceptions in determining the impact of one generation on another. These perceptions are not wholly accurate, nor are they subject only to random errors, which could be treated statistically if not at the level of individual cases. Instead, they are related in a complicated manner to family and personal characteristics and are a product of bias and systematic error as well as accurate views of parental attributes. Thus the role of youths' perceptions as a link in the transmission process between parent and child is hardly an obvious one, but it is potentially of considerable significance. The descriptive framework begun in this chapter should provide an opening wedge for an intensive analysis of that role.

4: Parents' Reports about Children's Partisanship

Studies of political socialization have often relied on respondents' reports of parental attributes. Seldom if ever has the procedure been reversed, so to speak, by asking parents about characteristics of their children.[1] In some ways this seems odd, since one procedure is such a natural extension of the other. However, despite the similarities of the two methods, asking parents about their children differs in some crucial respects from questioning offspring about their parents. New problems of a technical and interpretive nature are encountered. Although these problems are hardly insurmountable, they must still be overcome before parents' reports can be widely used. New types of findings will also emerge. In some cases children's and parents' reports about each other can be used in identical fashion. But certain uses of children's perceptions are not appropriate for parents' views, while new uses will take the place of those that must be discarded. In the first section of this chapter, we will consider some of the problems and prospects of relying on parental reports about children. Parents' reports about their children's partisanship will then be analyzed.[2]

1. In discussing children's reactions to the death of President Kennedy, Sigel (1965, p. 206) notes in passing that parents did not perceive the grief that children experienced. Almond and Verba (1963, pp. 132–43) asked parents about a hypothetical situation involving the marriage of a son or daughter within or across political party lines. For a nonpolitical example, see Hill and Hole (1958).

2. This chapter was originally drafted before the passage of the 18-year-old amendment. In light of the new voting age, parts of the chapter, especially the comments on participation opportunities for high school seniors, may seem outdated. However, two points should be kept in mind. First, many seniors are not 18 until some time into the school year. Since elections are usually held in the fall, most students cannot in fact vote until after they graduate. Secondly, the recent publicity about the youth vote,

PROBLEMS AND PROSPECTS

There are at least two potentially serious difficulties associated with the use of parents' reports about their children—problems of questionnaire construction and the possibility that parents' reports are incomplete and inaccurate. Problems relating to the design of questionnaires or interview schedules are created by the multiplicity of children for any set of parents and by their age variations.[3] Interview or questionnaire instructions for handling large families would be enormously complicated in order to be sure that a parent was responding about the proper child. Interviewing time might also be prohibitive for large families. Age variations of children raise problems about the applicability of survey questions. For example, parents can be asked about the voting behavior of their "child" if they have adult offspring; for preadults such questions would be inapplicable. Questions about political attitudes might properly be asked about youths, but for children below a certain age these inquiries are also inappropriate. In addition to making more complicated questionnaire formats, which probably increase the amount of error, the varying applicability of questions means that different amounts of information are available for children of various age groups if one begins with an adult sample.

The complexity of these problems should not be underestimated, but at the same time they are hardly insuperable. Experimentation with the procedure of asking adults about children could establish some guidelines about question wording, the applicability of questions, average length of interviews, and so on. Certain judicious decisions might also be made, such as asking about no more than

---

emphasizing the Independent status of young people, suggests that more parents could now be expected to know about their children's partisanship. However, if our discussion applies slightly less forcefully to high school seniors today, it would seem to be directly applicable to students earlier in high school.

3. I am thinking primarily of parents falling into samples drawn from adult populations. Some of the problems mentioned here can be avoided by the use of sample designs such as that used in the present study, in which the initial sample consists of children.

five children or arbitrarily inquiring only about children within a given age range. Problems of questionnaire design thus call for ingenuity and testing and should not unduly hamper attempts to ask parents about their children.

The second potential problem of using parental reports about children is whether parents know enough about the political attitudes and behavior of their offspring to provide a reasonable amount of information and whether their perceptions are sufficiently accurate to be of any use. While we grant that parents' reports *may be* incomplete and inaccurate, this possibility is no different conceptually from the same concern about children's reports. The accuracy of parents' reports is a matter for empirical determination and should not be judged a priori. Moreover, if parents are only dimly aware of youths' emerging political attitudes, this in itself is an important datum. Inability to report children's feelings and behavior accurately may prohibit certain uses of parental reports, but it also provides insights into the political socialization process, as will presently be seen. Finally, some parents would be asked about adult children. In these cases we can at least be sure that the "child" is old enough to have political attitudes.

The foregoing considerations lead directly to the questions of what uses can be made of parents' reports about their children and what can be learned thereby. If we leave aside for the moment the matter of empirical verification, there is no conceptual reason that parents' reports cannot be considered more or less accurate indicators of youths' attributes. If such an interpretation is empirically justified, parents' reports of their children can be used to study parent-child agreement in much the same way as children's reports of parents have been used. In fact, the use of parents' reports for this purpose would mean that a number of research avenues could be explored much more easily than otherwise. For example, it would permit researchers to study family influence on siblings while interviewing only a single respondent. Problems such as the homogeneity of brothers and sisters and the impact of parents on more than one child could be studied in this way. Families of varying sizes could also be studied with much less difficulty if each child did not have to be questioned. Another research problem that would be simplified by the use of parents as informants about children is the analysis of relationships among three generations. Parents could supply information about themselves, their parents, and their children. The economy of such a procedure is obvious.

The use of parents' reports about children is not limited to comparisons with parents' own attributes. Parents' reports of youths, like the youths' reports, can be considered perceptions that are subject to various kinds of error and bias. One's interest is then directed to the implications of these perceptions, such as they are, for the socialization process. Unlike youths' perceptions, parents' views are not part of the causal chain linking the two generations. They can, however, tell us a great deal about the process of political socialization in the family. Are parents aware of the developing social and political ideas of their children? Do they think instead of youths as essentially apolitical? Are daughters in particular thought to be uninterested in politics? Do parents think that their children share their own ideas or that they are rebelling against them? Do parents note differences among their children, or are brothers and sisters considered mostly similar? Answers to these questions will be helpful in understanding the extent to which the transmission of political values is purposive and intentional and the extent to which it is unintentional and even unconscious. If parents are largely unaware of youths' attitudes, it is unlikely that they are consciously trying to mold their children's political orientations.

The matter of intentional versus latent socialization can also be approached directly. Have parents tried to impress upon their children certain political or quasi-political ideas? Have they succeeded in doing so? Do parents care if their children's political opinions differ from their own? If so, what if anything have they done about it? Do they encourage or discourage their youngsters to be interested in public affairs? Answers to questions such as these will supplement inferences based on parents' knowledge about youths' political ideas.

My goal in this chapter is to provide an initial confrontation with both the methodological question of the completeness and accuracy of parent reports and the substantive question of what the findings tell us about the political socialization process. The analysis is limited to parents' reports of the party identification of their sons and daughters. Students' own reports of their partisan attitudes will be accepted as correct, for the same reasons set forth in introducing the concept in the last chapter.

Questions Used in This Study

Students and parents were asked about their own party loyalties using the standard SRC questions, as given in chapter 3. To ask the parents about their offspring, a preface was deemed necessary at the time the study was conducted to avoid an overwhelming response that "he isn't old enough to worry about politics yet." The question was worded:

> *Although your son (daughter) isn't old enough to participate in politics much, do you think he (she) would consider himself (herself) a Republican, a Democrat, an Independent, or what?*

The volunteered responses "hasn't decided yet" and "don't know" were accepted without further probing. No attempt was made to ascertain strength of partisanship or the partisan inclinations of Independents.

AGGREGATE COMPARISONS

The arguments suggesting that parents do or do not know youths' partisan loyalties represent something of a standoff. On the one hand, parents may not think of preadults as holding political attitudes and therefore may not be able to make even an educated guess about their child's partisanship. On the other hand, party identification is a sufficiently salient characteristic that parents might be expected to know at least this attribute of their high school senior.

The data support the first line of reasoning if it means that a large minority of the parents cannot identify their youths' partisan attitudes. Altogether 37 percent of the parents were unable to locate their child along the partisan spectrum. Parents expressed their lack of awareness in different terms. Twenty-six percent simply said that they did not know how the student felt, while another 11 percent said the student "hasn't decided yet." [4] The choices of wording (both of which were volunteered responses) are suggestive. The "hasn't decided" response, if taken literally, suggests that parents know something about the student's feelings. They know either that the student has simply not thought about partisan politics enough to judge the parties or that he or she has consciously considered the merits of the parties but has been unable to arrive at any decision (including the decision that the parties are about the same). The "don't know" (DK) response suggests a genuine lack of awareness on the part of the parent. Whatever partisan attitude the student has, if any, the parent is ignorant of it.

Despite the plausibility of these interpretations, no distinction between "hasn't decided" and DK responses will be made in the individual-level comparisons below. Although further investigation is clearly warranted, utilizing follow-up questions or interviewer probes to clarify parents' responses, I am not yet convinced that the choices of wording imply different levels of parental awareness. On the one hand, it is possible that for some parents a DK response really indicates that the parent does not think the student has made any partisan choice. On the other hand, some parents may use the "hasn't decided" response because it is less embarrassing than saying "I don't know." In any event, comparison of the relative frequency of the two responses in numerous subgroups of the population did not reveal any meaningful differences. The ratio of one response to the other is usually quite stable, and the rest of the time it fluctuates in an inconsistent pattern.

Among the 63 percent of the parents who attributed a party identification to their son or daughter, the aggregate distribution of the students was rather poorly estimated. A comparison of

4. By their own reports, only 1% of the students are undecided about their loyalties. Less than 0.5% said they were uninterested in politics or apolitical.

parent and student responses is provided in figure 4.1. Two sets of bars are given for students, one of which is based on all students while the other is based only on students to whom the parent attributed a party identification. The difference between the two student distributions is due to a higher rate of DK responses among parents of Independents.

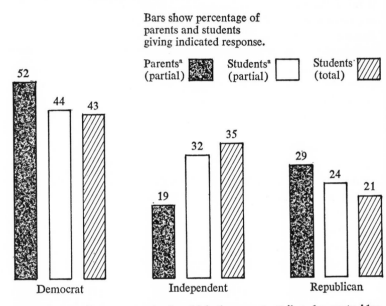

[a]Based on student-parent pairs in which the parent attributed a party identification to his son or daughter.

Figure 4.1
Aggregate Parent and Student Reports
of Student's Party Identification

The main discrepancy between parent and student reports is that parents grossly underestimate the proportion of youths who are Independents. This is true even if one ignores the effects of DK responses by comparing only the first two bars in each part of figure 4.1. Understating the proportion of Independents is the same type of error, although considerably enlarged here, that was noted in chapter 3, where students underestimated the number of Independent parents. However, here the error has the effect of obscuring generational differences. In fact, relying exclusively on parents' reports, one would conclude that students are less Independent or more partisan than their parents, while the opposite is true.

The division of partisan students into Democrats and Republicans is also incorrectly estimated using parents' reports. The error is not large in this case. Among all student partisans, 67 percent are Democrats, compared to 65 percent of the partisan parents. Parents' reports indicate that 64 percent of the student partisans appear to be Democrats, so that the true parent-student difference is slightly reversed. Discrepancies between parent and student estimates of the partisan division are also noticed among subgroups of the population. Sometimes, as above, the effect is to reverse the true student-parent difference, while in other instances the difference is underestimated but in the right direction.[5]

I defer to the next section a discussion of reasons for the inaccurate estimates given by parents of the distribution of party identification among the students and, in particular, for the very large underestimate of Independents. The discrepancies can be explained adequately only after observing accuracy rates at the level of parent-student pairs.

INDIVIDUAL COMPARISONS

As in the aggregate comparisons, the initial focus here will be on variations in the proportion of parents who claim not to know their child's partisan attitudes. After a discussion of these variations, attention will be given to the accuracy rate among parents who do attribute party loyalties to their children. The extent to

5. An interesting example of discrepancies within subgroups is found by controlling on region. In the South the parents are more Democratic than the students; in the non-South the parents are less Democratic. In each case, however, parents' reports underestimate generational differences. Democrats, as a percentage of Democrats plus Republicans, are represented (in percentages) as follows:

	South	Non-South
All students	73.0	66.0
Students as reported by parents	75.0	59.5
All parents	78.0	59.5

which the proportion of DKs and the rate of accuracy covary will also be noted.[6]

The relationships between a number of control variables and the proportion of parents unable to identify their youths' partisan feelings are given in table 4.1. As expected, parents are most often unable to classify Independent students, but the pattern of DKs

Table 4.1
Percentage of Parents Unaware of Student's
Party Identification, within Control Categories[a]

Control Category	Percent DK[a]	N	Control Category		Percent DK[a]	N
Student's party identification			*Level of family politicization*			
Strong Dem.	34	359	High	1	25	182
Weak Dem.	38	457		2	31	323
Ind. Dem.	37	274		3	37	418
Ind.	51	242		4	38	350
Ind. Rep.	45	158		5	49	232
Weak Rep.	36	258	Low	6	45	158
Strong Rep.	18	143	*Sex combinations*			
Region			Mother-son		35	707
Northeast	40	464	Mother-daughter		37	644
Midwest	38	581	Father-son		39	574
South	36	542	Father-daughter		38	518
West	36	328	*Parent respondent*			
Race			Natural parent		37	1,816
White	37	1,717	Stepparent			
Black	44	199	or surrogate		48	99

[a] Includes parents who responded "don't know" and "hasn't decided yet."

within categories of the students' party identification is less regular and not as strong as supposed. Parents label Independent Democrats just as often as weak Democrats and both of those nearly as often as strong identifiers of that party. On the Republican side the variations are monotonic and sharper, but even then over a third of the weak identifiers were not labeled by parents.

6. In the remainder of the chapter "don't know" or DK responses refer to parents who said they do not know their youths' partisan attitudes and those who said that the students had not made up their minds.

The erratic pattern of DKs within party identification categories is partially due to the effects of other variables given in table 4.1. Blacks, for example, who are labeled by parents less often than whites, tend to raise the proportion of DKs among strong Democratic identifiers but not among other students. Among white strong Democrats, the proportion of DKs drops to 31 percent. Family politicization also contributes to the erratic pattern. In particular, it helps account for the small number of DK responses among parents of strong Republican identifiers. Strong Republicans are considerably more politicized than any other group, which makes their partisan attachments more salient. It ought to be observed, however, that a rather uneven pattern of DKs within party identification categories is maintained for all levels of politicization.

Politicization of the family is itself significantly related to the proportion of parents who do not know their youths' party identification. Fully one-quarter of the parents are unable to label their children when both parent and student report frequent political conversations, but this is much less than the nearly 50 percent DK rate among the least politicized families. It should be noted, for reference below, that measures of the parents' and students' political interest were also related to the proportion of DK responses. As the political interest expressed by the parents or students increased, the proportion of DKs decreased steadily. One other measure, labeled by Milbrath (1965, pp. 155–56) as a campaign activity index, was not monotonically related to the proportion of DKs, but it did show that parents who were very inactive were able to label their youths' feelings much less often than parents who were more highly involved.

Of the other variables examined, the only one that reveals the expected relationship to parents' claims of knowledge is whether the parent respondent was a natural parent or a parent substitute. About 11 percent fewer of the stepparents or surrogates were able to identify the students' party loyalties. There is a difference in the proportion of DKs between whites and blacks, but the direction is mildly surprising. It might have been expected that black parents would say that their children were Democratic (as

96 percent of them are) even if they really did not know.[7] The tendency to assume that students are Democrats might also have been expected to lower the proportion of DKs in the South, but regional differences are minimal. Almost no differences at all are observed among parent-student sex combinations. Parents are no less likely to know their daughters' than their sons' partisan feelings and mothers label their children as often as fathers. Finally, data not shown reveal no meaningful differences in the proportion of DK responses for families of various sizes and for younger or older parents.

The rate of accuracy among parents who do attribute partisan loyalties to their children is quite high. The correlation between parent and student reports is .57, which is nearly identical to the correlation obtained using students' reports of parents.[8] Further insight into the parents' reports is provided by the data in table 4.2, which shows the accuracy of parental reports within categories of party identification. The pattern observed in the table is highly similar to that noted for students' reports. Accuracy is higher for partisans, especially strong identifiers, than for Independents. Among Independent leaners the rate of accuracy is particularly low, but the partisan inclinations of the students are accurately perceived. Reports of strong and weak Democrats are more accurate than reports of Republican identifiers.

Comparison of table 4.2 and table 3.3 reveals that there are almost no differences in parent and student reports of partisans. Among weak Republican identifiers the parents are correct somewhat less often, but this is partially balanced by a slightly smaller proportion who reportedly identify with the Democrats. Among

7. The higher rate of DKs among blacks is not due to the greater proportion of parent surrogates among them. In black families with one or both natural parents the proportion of DKs (45%) is just as high as for all blacks.

8. All of the correlations in this chapter are based on 3 × 3 tables. Since parent reports of youths yielded only the 3 major categories, the choice was between 7 × 3 or 3 × 3 tables, and the latter was uniformly adopted. Usually both tables give very similar results. In the comparisons made, the difference was no greater than .02 in all but one instance. In that case (blacks, where the difference is .08), the correlation is not cited anyway because the distribution is so skewed (there being few black Independents and almost no Republicans).

Table 4.2
Parent and Student Reports of Student's Party Identification
(In percentages)

Parent's Report			Student's Report				
	Strong Dem.	*Weak Dem.*	*Ind. Dem.*	*Ind.*	*Ind. Rep.*	*Weak Rep.*	*Strong Rep.*
Democrat	90	75	58	36	7	12	11
Independent	7	16	28	40	34	22	4
Republican	3	8	14	24	59	66	84
Total	100	99	100	100	100	100	99
N	237	284	173	118	87	166	118

NOTE: This table is based only on parents who attributed a party identification to their son or daughter.

all three categories of Independents, parents' reports are less accurate than students'. The remarks in chapter 3 about the difficulty that parents might encounter in conveying an Independent image are apparently even more applicable to youths. With fewer opportunities to express their partisan attitudes, youths have little chance of displaying the view that the virtues of one party are balanced by its weaknesses or by virtues of the other party. It should be noted that the partisan inclinations of Independents are perceived at least as accurately by parents as by students. This is shown by the relatively few parents who classify Independent leaners as partisans of the "wrong" party.

It was remarked earlier that the inaccurate aggregate estimate given by parents of the youths' party loyalties could be explained adequately only after observing accuracy rates within student-parent pairs. Part of the explanation should now be obvious. The low rates of accuracy among Independent students meant that many of them were not labeled at all or were misclassified; at the same time, the high accuracy rates among student partisans meant that this "loss" of Independents was not balanced by an equal number of partisans who were erroneously reported as Independents. The same phenomenon, however, was observed in students' reports of parents, and yet the aggregate differences in that case were not too large. Admittedly, student reports were somewhat more accurate among Independents than parent reports. But those differences hardly seem large enough to explain the much greater aggregate discrepancies noted in this chapter.

The additional factor contributing to the larger aggregate differences observed here is the distribution of students (by their own reports) along the party identification spectrum. More of the students than the parents considered themselves nonpartisan, so that the low rates of accuracy among Independents created a greater distortion in reports given (by parents) about the students. A convincing demonstration of this can be made by supposing that the students were distributed among the party identification categories in the same way as parents. In other words, suppose the distribution of students was Democrats 49 percent, Independents 24 percent, Republicans 27 percent. By simple algebraic procedures, utilizing the proportion of parents who gave DK responses within party identification categories (table 4.1) and the proportion classifying students in each category (table 4.2), we can figure out what the distribution of students according to parents' reports *would have been* under the given assumption.[9] It turns out that the parents would have given a distribution as follows: Democrats 54 percent, Independents 17 percent, Republicans 29 percent. The average difference between these figures and the assumed student distribution is 4.7 percent. This is less than half of the difference of 11.0 percent observed in figure 4.1.

This example explains the large aggregate discrepancies observed in parental reports of the students' party identification. It is also a concrete illustration of the theoretical possibility pointed

9. The procedure is as follows. First, the proportion of "students" in each of the 7 party identification categories is multiplied by the proportion of parents within each category who attributed a partisan attitude to their son or daughter. Second, the 7 figures resulting from the first step are added and each is divided by the total. (This yields the distribution along the party identification spectrum of the cases in which the parent was not DK; it is analogous to the "partial" student bars of figure 4.1.) Third, the proportion in each category as a result of the second step is multiplied successively by the proportion of parents who report those students as Democrats, Independents, and Republicans, and is cumulated across the 7 categories. The final result shows the aggregate distribution of students as given by parents that would have existed under the given assumption.

out in chapter 3 (note 10). It was noted there that it is a disadvantage, methodologically speaking, for accuracy rates for a given variable to depend on the particular categorization of the respondent, because aggregate differences will be very large for some distributions of the sample on that variable. Here, variations in accuracy rates within categories of party identification, together with the overall distribution of students' party loyalties, have resulted in rather large aggregate errors—even though at the *individual level* parents' reports are just as accurate as students' reports of parents. Casual use of parents' reports to determine the aggregate distribution of youths' partisan attitudes is therefore misleading at best and will possibly lead to totally false conclusions. Fortunately, the data presented here can shed some light on the magnitude of this problem in other research contexts (see chap. 7).

Other variations in the accuracy of parents' reports will be discussed summarily. In many cases variations do occur, but they are not large, nor necessarily in the expected direction. For example, a number of characteristics of the family do not consistently affect accuracy rates. The correlation between parent and student reports is nearly identical for families with one or two natural parents and families in which a stepparent or surrogate was interviewed. The number of children in the family and the age of the parent are unrelated to the accuracy of parental reports. Correlations within combinations of parent-student sex show that mothers do give less accurate reports about their sons ($\tau_b = $ .53), but their reports about daughters are the most accurate of all (.60). Fathers' reports are equally accurate for sons (.57) and for daughters (.58). Among regions of the country, parents' reports are least accurate in the South (.53). This is due principally to the inaccuracy of reports given by non-Democratic blacks (see below). Among Southern whites the correlation is .57. Accuracy is highest in the Northeast (.63), with somewhat lower rates in the Midwest (.57) and the West (.55).

It is logical to suppose that the accuracy of parents' reports, like those of students, should vary directly with the level of family politicization. However, the evidence concerning this relationship is mixed. Using the family politicization index based on husband-wife and student-parent political conversations, we find the following parent-student correlations, running from the most to least politicized families: .67, .60, .56, .49, .66, .44. The strong, monotonic pattern is ruined only by the disturbingly high correlation in the fifth category. It is tempting to try to "explain away" this single disturbance. And there are two factors that boost the correlation by a small amount.[10] But there are other indications that levels of politicization may not have a systematic effect on parent reports. The accuracy of parent reports was observed within the categories of three variables that might be said to measure individual politicization. Two items asked about the parents' and the students' interest in public affairs and politics, while the third was a measure of active parental participation. It was observed earlier that these variables were consistently related to the proportion of DKs in parent reports. They were also monotonically related to the accuracy of students' reports of parents' party identification. Of these three variables, only one (student interest) systematically affected the correlation between parent and student reports. For the other two, the correlations fluctuated with no apparent pattern. Hence the effect of family and individual politicization on the accuracy of parent reports remains unclear.

Self-directed Bias in Parents' Reports

Self-directed bias influences parents' reports of students more significantly than it affects youths' reports about parents. This conclusion is based on a comparison of the true student-parent correlation with that obtained by using parents' reports of the

10. As noted in table 4.1 above, the fifth category has the highest rate of DK responses. This means that a number of respondents who are especially likely to give inaccurate reports are not entered in the table on which the correlation is based. However, the proportion of DKs in this fifth category is only 4% above that among the least politicized, so that this factor probably raises the correlation very little. Examination of the distribution of party identification within each of the 6 groups reveals that there were slightly fewer Independents in the fifth category. Since Independents are less accurately perceived, this tends to raise the parent-student correlation. However, if we assume that the distribution of students in the fifth category was the same as in the sixth, the "adjusted" value of the correlation is still .63.

students. This is done for the total sample in the top portion of figure 4.2. The correct parent-student correlation is given on the

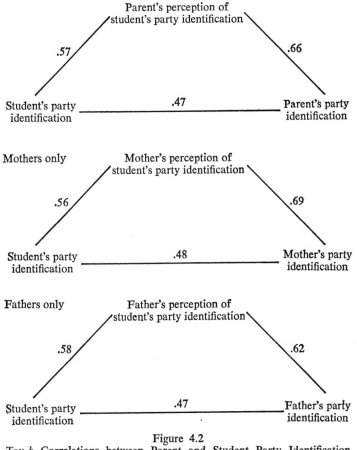

Figure 4.2
Tau-*b* Correlations between Parent and Student Party Identification
Using Parents' Perceptions of Students and Students' Own Reports

bottom line of the triangle. The estimate of this relationship based on parents' reports of students is on the upper-right diagonal.[11]

11. In order to make figure 4.2 directly comparable to figure 3.4, the parent's and student's party identification have been reversed.

On the third side of the triangle, the correlation between parents' perceptions and students' own reports is repeated as a convenience. The use of parents' reports overestimates the true parent-student correlation by .19, which is about twice the overestimate for the three variables observed in the last chapter.

In the student reports, the amount of self-directed bias was almost identical in the case of mothers and fathers. This was not true of parents. Of the inaccurate reports by mothers, 70 percent were in the direction of the mothers' own partisan attitude, whereas for fathers the comparable figure is 64 percent. The effects of this differential bias are observed in the lower portion of figure 4.2. Mothers' reports overestimate the true student-parent correlation by a particularly large margin, although the overestimate based on fathers' reports is still larger than that based on students' reports of parents.[12]

Self-directed bias, combined with distributional properties of subpopulations, also helps explain certain interesting patterns observed in parent reports. One such finding is that black youths who claimed to be Independents were usually reported as Democratic whereas inaccurate reports of white Independents were more evenly divided between the parties. A similar pattern was observed in the last chapter for youths' reports about parents. The tendency to report parents as Democratic was observed even among students who were themselves non-Democratic. It was suggested there that because of their expectations black youths usually saw their parents as Democratic regardless of their professed beliefs. Here, however, if one controls for the parents' own partisan attitude, the difference between the races nearly vanishes. For example, among white and black Democratic parents, youths who are Independents were classified as Democrats in about the same proportions. Among Independent and Republican parents (combined to increase the number of cases) there is, if anything, a slightly lesser tendency for black parents to re-

12. To get some idea of the distribution of overestimates for subgroups of the population, we applied here the same 5 controls that were used in connection with the student reports. For the 20 control categories, the mean overestimate was .17. Except for one extreme value of .03, all of the overestimates were in the range .12–.24.

port their youths as Democrats. Thus the overall racial difference is an artifact of the disproportionate number of Democratic
parents among blacks compared to whites.[13] Reports of both races
are subject to rather similar amounts of self-directed bias.

The explanation for the differences between blacks and whites
is based partly on a very small number of cases, so it should
be regarded as suggestive rather than conclusive. Additional support is provided, however, by the viability of a similar explanation
for another significant finding. Outside the South, Democratic and
Republican students are perceived with about the same rate of
accuracy. Among Southerners, on the other hand, Democratic
students are very accurately perceived whereas Republicans are
more often incorrectly identified. This striking difference is shown
in table 4.3. One obvious explanation of this regional contrast is

Table 4.3
Parent and Student Reports of Student's Party Identification, by Region
(In percentages)

| Parent's Report | Student's Report | | | | | |
| | *South* | | | *Non-South* | | |
	Dem.	*Ind.*	*Rep.*	*Dem.*	*Ind.*	*Rep.*
Democrat	91	39	27	78	38	6
Independent	6	36	14	15	32	15
Republican	2	25	59	7	30	79
Total	99	100	100	100	100	100
N	128	80	71	313	273	209

NOTE: This table is based only on parents who attributed a party identification
to their son or daughter. Only white families are included.

that Southern parents assume that their children identify with
the dominant party of the region; even among students who say
they are Republicans, a large minority of parents think that the
youths have just absorbed the predominant Southern attitude.
Further investigation shows that this is a superficial and misleading explanation. Controlling for the parents' own partisanship
virtually eliminates the difference between the South and the non-

13. Among student Democrats, the proportion of Democratic parents is
only slightly higher for blacks than for whites. Accordingly there is no difference in the accuracy of reporting black and white Democratic students.

South. In both regions self-directed bias is equally observable. For example, among Democratic parents, students who consider themselves Democrats are perceived just as accurately in the South as elsewhere; students who say they are Independent or Republican are wrongly labeled Democratic in nearly identical proportions in the two regions. Hence, it is only the greater proportion of Democratic parents in the South that leads to the overall difference.[14]

The empirical evidence presented here strongly recommends against the use of parents' reports as accurate indicators of youths' partisan attitudes. This conclusion rests on three principal findings: (1) over a third of the parents were unable to identify their youths' party loyalties; (2) the aggregate student distribution was poorly reproduced in parental reports (and the generally higher proportion of Independents among young people suggests that this would typically be the case); and (3) self-directed bias exerted considerable influence on parents' reports.

Unlike the conclusions reached in other chapters, extension of the present findings to other situations seems to be straightforward. Political variables other than partisan attitudes and any political information about young children are likely to be reported very poorly by parents. The saliency of party identification compared to other attitudinal variables was discussed in the last chapter. It follows that if partisan feelings are not reported completely and accurately, reports of other political attitudes and orientations are likely to be even more inadequate. When the desired information concerns children younger than high school seniors, the proportion of DK responses will undoubtedly increase. If many parents do not know the political attitudes of youths who are nearing adulthood, very large proportions will be ignorant of the developing attitudes of younger children. It is still possible that parents can provide adequate information about adult off-

14. Of course this explanation in no way negates the differences observed in table 4.3. Students in the South and non-South are still perceived with differing levels of accuracy.

spring, but having open only this single avenue seriously restricts the use of imaginative research designs.

In contrast to their questionable value as indicators of youths' actual feelings, parents' reports do seem useful as an indicator of some aspects of the socialization process. At least two major substantive conclusions can be drawn from the current findings. First of all, they suggest that the process of socialization into partisan orientations is carried on nearly at a subconscious level. It is not much of an exaggeration to say the parents socialize their children despite themselves. Certainly the parents who do not know their children's party identification and those who think that their children have not yet made up their minds are not intentionally directing the development of their children's political ideas. If they were attempting to exercise deliberate influence, the children's current feelings would be the very first information they would seek. For the two-thirds of the parents who do attribute a party identification to their son or daughter, the possibility that they are consciously directing their youths' attitudes cannot be ruled out entirely. However, this possibility can be discounted on other grounds. The fact that parents often do not accurately perceive their children's preferences suggests that they have a very shaky basis for attempting to influence them. That parents have not always conveyed their own preferences to their youths also suggests a lack of effort on their part. Among most parents the process of political socialization is a remote concern.

The other substantive conclusion suggested by the findings is that parents by and large do not care what their children's partisan orientations are.[15] This seems to follow directly from the first conclusion. If youths' partisan attitudes were important to parents, they would make a greater attempt to influence their development in desired directions. But if parents are mostly indifferent to the party loyalties of youths, there is no particular

15. This is similar to the conclusion reached by Almond and Verba (1963, p. 135) that "overwhelming majorities of the respondents of both parties [in the United States but not in other countries] expressed indifference regarding the partisan affiliations of the future mates of their children."

reason for them to even be aware of what their children think. It might be argued that parents *seem* unconcerned because they assume that children simply follow in parents' footsteps. There is some validity in this argument since parents did bias their views of student attitudes toward their own feelings. But the proportion of DKs and the extent of bias hardly support the conclusion that parents assume children accept their views unquestioningly. Hence many parents must be relatively indifferent to the partisan orientations of their children.

We hasten to add that the lack of deliberate efforts to direct the socialization of youths in partisan directions does not mean that such efforts are lacking on all political and social matters. Parents are concerned about their children's attitudes regarding basic societal rules, such as obeying the law, being loyal to one's country, etc. At times there are also less consensual topics on which parents try to influence children's views. One thinks, for example, of the civil rights issue, which for some people is a moral or religious matter as well as a social concern. When contemporary events bring such an emotionally charged issue to the fore, parents may feel called upon to guide their children's views as much as possible.

An additional qualification of the present conclusions is that parents' lack of concern about youths' partisan attitudes, as well as political attitudes more generally, is not unlimited. Parents may be totally indifferent about their children's political views—so long as they do not become ———(socialists, communists, John Birchers, Ku Klux Klansmen, Yippies, pacifists, etc.). The blank is filled in variously by different people. For some the bounds of political acceptability may be very narrow and for others rather wide. But for most parents we suggest that there are limits between which they attempt to guide their children. The limits may be fuzzy, of course, and they certainly change over periods of history. Moreover, in many and perhaps most cases parents have to provide little explicit direction to guide youths along the desired paths; the efforts of other socialization agencies and the example of parents' own attitudes and actions are a sufficient force. Nevertheless, parents do try to insure that their children develop within certain bounds. It remains the task of future

research efforts to discover the types of political or social concerns on which parents feel the need to influence their children's
views, how narrow or broad the bands of acceptability are, and
what, if any, explicit efforts are made by parents to insure that
youths' attitudes fall within these boundaries.

5: Family Structure and Relationships among Family Members

Family power structure and affective relationships within the family lie at the heart of much theorizing about the role of the family in the socialization process (Schaefer, 1961; Straus, 1964; Walters and Stinnett, 1971). The distribution of power among family members affects youngsters in a multiplicity of ways— most notably, for the political scientist, by introducing to them the concept of power and by developing their understanding of power relationships. Feelings of attachment and affection within the family are presumably related to processes of role modeling and imitation of parental behavior as well as helping determine levels of family interaction. For present purposes we will also consider a third dimension—the amount of agreement or disagreement among members of the family. Although intrafamilial agreement is no doubt related, as both cause and effect, to affective relationships, it is more specific in nature and more limited in scope. It is important as a determinant of the uniformity of stimuli reaching the child and possibly of the type of interaction among family members.

Empirical research has also relied heavily on these characteristics of the family. Psychologists and sociologists have studied the effect of family power structure on children's aggressiveness (Kagen, 1958), leadership behavior (Bronfenbrenner, 1961), and peer group adjustment (Hoffman, 1961), while affectivity has been related to the development of self-esteem (Rosenberg, 1965, pp. 42–46) and leadership qualities (Bronfenbrenner, 1961). Political scientists and their allies have relied on power structure and affectivity in various combinations to help explain rebellion against parents (Middleton and Putney, 1963; Lane, 1959; Maccoby et al., 1954), feelings of political competence (Almond and Verba, 1963; chap. 12), and adolescents' and adults' political interest (Langton, 1969, chap. 2; Hess and Torney, 1965, p. 200; Lane, 1959). Questions about intrafamily agreement have been used in a general way to distinguish areas of consensus and conflict (Blood and Wolfe, 1960, pp. 239–51). Political scientists have examined parental agreement specifically as it is related to the transmission of party loyalties from parents to children (McClosky and Dahlgren, 1959; Campbell et al., 1960, p. 147; Jennings and Niemi, 1974).

Despite the frequent, multidisciplinary use of these family characteristics in theory and research, little effort has been made to validate the measures used as indicators of them. In this chapter I make one approach to the problem by comparing student and parent responses to a series of questions about family structure and interaction.[1] Unlike earlier chapters, the interpretation of results hinges partly on the comparable analysis of husbands' and wives' reports in part 2. An interpretation of the results will thus be put off until chapter 8.

NATURE OF THE DATA

The family, or any element of structure or any relationship in it, is not a single, undifferentiated object that can be observed and characterized with nearly perfect precision. Of particular importance is the fact that the family is a multiplicity of roles and relationships and is not perceived identically by all of its members. Each member does not partake of every action of every other family member. Nor is every aspect of the relationship between certain members observed by all of the others. It follows that different members do not view the family in precisely the same way, and their descriptions of it cannot be expected to match perfectly.

It is obvious, then, that some discrepancies will occur in the reports of different family members. However, it is often im-

---

1. Straus (1969, p. 7) concludes that a majority of the instruments he surveyed show no substantial evidence of validity. Particularly in regard to the approach used here, it is interesting to note that very few of the 319 measurement techniques catalogued by Straus compare reports from multiple family members.

plicitly assumed that the intrafamily experiences of different members are sufficiently overlapping that all characterize the family in similar ways. While no two members view *exactly* the same family interaction, there is a large common element to their experiences, so that in most cases reports about the family will be very similar regardless of which member is the respondent.[2] This argument seems especially appropriate when family members are reporting about interaction in which they are involved. For example, it may be true that children incorrectly perceive the relationship between the mother and father because they do not observe all aspects of husband-wife interaction. But they can still accurately report relationships between themselves and other family members.

A second conceptual point that must be clarified at the outset is the meaning of student-parent (and later, husband-wife) agreement. If a high level of agreement is found between students' and parents' reports, it would not conclusively demonstrate that respondents give accurate information about the family. Neither the students' nor the parents' reports can be considered a standard by which to judge the accuracy of the others' perceptions. It is entirely possible that both students' and parents' reports do not accurately reflect the true family situation. In fact, it is for this reason that I shall speak in this chapter of student-parent "agreement" rather than of the "accuracy" of student or parent reports. Technically, then, we cannot determine here whether students' or parents' reports are accurate pictures of family life. Nevertheless, if considerable student-parent agreement is found, it would strengthen the view that respondents do give reasonably accurate reports of family living. Conversely, if little student-parent agreement is discovered, it definitely shows that respondents' reports cannot be relied upon for accurate descriptions of the true family situation (at least without independent verification). Since the reports of one set of respondents are disputed by those of other

2. Another point of view is that while the interaction observed by different family members is not identical, the same *type* of behavior is observed by everyone. For example, if the mother dominates the decision making that is observed by a given member, she probably dominates decision making seen by other members as well.

family members, there is no way of knowing which, if either, set of respondents is giving accurate reports, unless one set of responses can be verified by some method that does not rely on family members' reports.

It should be pointed out that some researchers concede that different family members give varying reports but feel that this is quite irrelevant. According to this point of view, it is the *perceptions* of the family that are important and not the real structure or relationships. For example, if a family member thinks that he gets along with other members very poorly, this perception is what affects his attitudes and behavior; it is not important how other family members judge his relationship to them nor how these relationships might be characterized by some objective measure. I agree that this argument is sometimes valid. The problem, however, is that theoretical attempts to link the family with dependent variables are often specified in behavioral rather than cognitive terms. Thus while it is argued that only perceptions are important, hypotheses and explanations of findings are given in terms that imply knowledge of factual information about the family. Moreover, attempts to alter family features will be rendered more difficult if we are dealing with perceptions only partially related to objective characteristics. In any event, I will put aside this argument of perceptions versus facts until I interpret our findings at the end of chapter 8, where I will deal with the problem at greater length.

To set the stage for the analysis, a brief review is made of previous studies in which the validity of family-level data has been questioned. They suggest particular types of disagreements and biases that should concern us here.

Validity of Family-Level Data: Previous Studies

Most studies that have questioned the validity of respondents' reports about the family have done just that; they have questioned the reports and suggested possible biases, but they have not been able to test their ideas. Often these questions are raised in opening paragraphs along with other caveats about the quality of the data or appear as closing comments qualifying the results. Nevertheless, the concern is genuine. Typical of this concern is Havighurst's and Davis' remark that "to an unknown extent, mothers give what they regard as 'expected' or 'appropriate' answers when telling how they raise their children" (1955, p. 441).

This quotation summarizes what seem to be the predominant feelings that have been expressed about children's and parents' reports about the family. First is the almost unanimous suspicion that reports are biased, if at all, in the direction of socially desirable responses. Miller and Swanson (1958, p. 88), for example, suggest that mothers respond to questions about child rearing in terms of ideal practices rather than actual behavior. Radke (1946) suspects a similar bias, especially because the parents in her sample are well educated and would be amply aware of "expert" child-training standards. Cass feels that parents' responses to attitude questions are likewise colored by a desire "to appear in good light" (1952, p. 307).[3]

The second predominant belief is that children's reports are less biased than parents'.[4] This is often coupled with the suggestion that children are better reporters, even about parental behavior. Herbst (1952) feels that children may be better informants than parents on a series of questions about parents' daily activities. Parents may give an impression of greater cooperation and agreement than really exists. Helpter (1958) suggests that children's reports of parental evaluations of children may be more accurate than evaluations by the parents themselves because children perceive attitudes which parents do not acknowledge. Ausubel et al. note that children may give more valid responses, particularly when the subjects are emotionally laden, because "the intent of

3. Many other studies could be cited. See, for example, Smith (1958), Hoffman (1957), Epstein and Komorita (1965), Yarrow et al. (1968, pp. 137–40), and some of the references given by Hess and Torney (1963). If the necessity of recalling past behavior is also imposed, even factual information about child rearing may be poorly reported. See Goddard et al. (1961), Chess et al. (1960), and Wenar (1961). For a slightly different type of question, Schramm et al. (1961, p. 215) note that mothers may have underestimated their children's television watching because they were ashamed of the amount of television the children saw.

4. However, it is sometimes said that children's reports are also biased toward socially approved answers. See Kagen (1956) and Maxwell et al. (1961).

such inquiries can be more effectively disguised from children and because of their relative inexperience in such matters" (1954, pp. 173–74).

Only a few studies have actually been able to compare the reports of children and parents. They have usually shown a serious lack of agreement. Hess and Torney (1963) obtained written questionnaires along with interview material from four members in each of forty-four families (mother, father, two children). Family power structure was measured by interviewers' ratings and by resolution of revealed differences, in addition to a number of interview questions. They conclude that the method of gathering information and the format of the items are important sources of variation. Most interesting, however, are their contrasting findings about aggregate and individual comparisons: "Fathers, mothers, and children, as groups, show a high level agreement in their attitudes toward the role performance and power relationships of family members. Despite these marked similarities between groups, there is little agreement among members of most families" (p. 13). Maxwell et al. (1961), in a study of fifty tenth graders and their parents, also found similar aggregate reports. When differences were found, the students gave more favorable responses slightly more often than parents.

Two other studies provide data which, though incidental to the larger goals of the work, reveal discrepancies in reports of different family members. Kohn and Carroll (1960) sampled eighty-two families (mother, father, fifth grade child) for a study of the allocation of parental responsibilities by different social classes. One aspect of the study concerned the student-parent relationship or "who the student turned to." They found that in about 40 percent of the families, all three members agreed on the relationship between student and parents. In about a third of the families the mother and father agreed, but the child differed in his assessment, while in the remaining quarter of the families the child and one parent disagreed with the other parent. The authors' interesting explanation for the observed differences will be discussed below.

The other study, which is also by Hess and Torney (1965, 1967), is part of an inquiry into socialization during the elementary school years. Questionnaire data were gathered from a large sample of youngsters, which included about 200 pairs of siblings. The younger child in each pair of siblings was matched with an unrelated child of the same school, grade, sex, and social status of his older brother or sister. Correlations were then obtained between responses of siblings and of matched pairs in order to observe whether the similarity of siblings' reports exceeded that of the unrelated individuals. Several of the items related to the family setting, such as the parents' interest in government, the parents' role in citizenship training, and some personality traits of the father. On these items, the correlations between siblings' reports, while usually higher than for the matched pairs, were remarkably low. Children from the same family are clearly not giving identical reports. Hess and Torney tersely conclude: "Obviously, two children's views of their family are not determined solely by its realistic characteristics" (1965, p. 194).[5]

The suggestions and findings of these studies are useful in two ways. First, they emphasize the need to look for generational differences in the responses of the student and parent samples. That is, do students' reports vary systematically from parents', perhaps giving a less harmonious and more discordant picture of family life? Or do we find numerous crosscutting effects so that in some families students' observations vary in one direction from parents', while in other families the direction is reversed? In either case intrafamily consensus may be just as lacking, but the interpretation and implications of the findings would be quite different. Second, since the several studies that compared multiple samples utilized children of varying ages, they provide some kind of basis for generalizing the results of the present analysis. Specifically, they suggest that the lack of agreement which will be shown between reports of high school seniors and their parents is not due to the use of this particular student cohort.

5. In a number of other studies just the husband's and wife's reports were compared. They often show more disagreement than agreement. For references, see chapter 8.

Questions Used in This Study

The variety of operational measures of family power, affection, and agreement prompted us to ask several questions relating to each dimension. In particular, questions were asked both about the parent(s) alone and about the parent(s) and child. In all but one instance the questions were worded identically in the parent and student interviews except for references to other family members (e.g., "father" versus "husband," "parents" versus "son" or "daughter"). To avoid another possible contaminating factor the parent interviews were structured so that questions about their "child" clearly referred to the son or daughter who had recently been interviewed.

The distribution of power between husband and wife was ascertained by a general question and by two items regarding specific decisions:[6]

> *Here's a list of ways of making family decisions.*[7] (Respondent was given a card with the following responses: Father makes decisions, Mother makes decisions, Parents act together, Each parent acts individually.) *By and large, how are decisions made in your family?*
> *How about decisions on the punishment of children for misbehavior? How are these decisions made?* (Same card) *How about on deciding how to vote in elections? How are these decisions made?* (Same card)

For the first two questions the "together" and "individually" responses will sometimes be combined and treated as a middle category between father dominance and mother dominance. For the voting question, virtually all parents and students reported individual or collaborative decision making, and all statistics

6. The questions are given only as worded in the student interview. For purposes of comparability, these and some of the other questions were taken directly from Almond and Verba (1963).

7. Obviously some of the questions—for example, those about conjugal power structure—were inappropriate for the approximately 11% of the students not living with two parents. Only students with two parents will be used in calculating percentages or summary statistics for those questions.

based on this question will use only these two categories. Both samples were also asked to describe the distribution of power between parents and students, and in a follow-up question, they were asked to appraise the power distribution:

> *In your case does your family want to have quite a lot to say about your friends and the places you go, and so on, or are you pretty much on your own?* (The volunteered response of "about average" was coded as a third response.)
> *Do you think they have too much to say, too little to say, or is it about right?*

The affectivity dimension was tapped by several questions. The first item refers to student-parent relations (taking each parent separately), while the second deals with the husband and wife alone:

> *How close would you say you are to your father (mother)— very close, pretty close, or not very close? Compared with other families you know, would you say that your mother and father get along with each other extremely well, not so well, or about average?*

Another question, based on the assumption that parent-student relations fluctuate during adolescence, called for a comparison with previous feelings:

> *Compared with how you get along with your parent(s) now, would you say that three years ago you got along with them (him) (her) better, worse, or about the same?*

Follow-up questions asked why students and parents got along better or worse now.

Two questions dealt with disagreements among family members. The question about student-parent disagreement is general in nature:

> *Are there any important things about which you and your parent(s) disagree?* (If yes) *What sorts of things would that be?*

The question about husband-wife differences refers specifically to political matters; however, comparison of student and parent responses is complicated by the use of somewhat different formats. Students were asked:

> *As far as you know, do your parents pretty much agree on public affairs and political matters, or do they disagree on some of these things?*

Parents were asked if they ever discussed political affairs with their spouse; the 80 percent who answered affirmatively to this preliminary question were then asked:

> *Do you and your wife (husband) ever disagree about anything having to do with public affairs and politics? (If yes) Would you say that you disagree frequently, occasionally, or seldom?*

For comparison with students, parents who "never disagree" or who "disagree, but seldom" will be coded as agreeing. Parents who "don't talk about politics" will be excluded since there is little basis for determining agreement.

Two other items, used in only one place below, concerned attention to programs about public affairs, politics, and the news on television and radio. After screening questions removed those who seldom use the media, each sample was asked:

> *Do you usually watch (listen) with other members of your family, or mostly by yourself?*

Only pairs in which both the student and parent survived the screening questions were used.[8]

AGGREGATE COMPARISONS

Comparison of aggregate response patterns gives one good indication of the generational character of discrepancies in reports

---

8. Students and parents rarely said they were unable to answer questions about the family. "Don't know" responses rose above 1% of the sample only once, and then only to 1.5%. Even when parents were asked about their families as they were growing up, almost no one volunteered a DK response.

of students and parents. If there are systematic differences in the way students and parents view the family, there should be impressive differences in the aggregate responses of the two samples. In contrast, high rates of individual-level agreement or numerous crosscutting effects would result in similar reports on the group level.

In the aggregate the pictures of family life given by students and parents are very similar. The marginal distributions for the two samples usually differ by less than 10 percent for any response category. The gross outlines of family living are the same according to both generations. At the same time, students regularly report slightly less harmony and somewhat more friction in family relations. Three general conclusions can be drawn:

1. Students less frequently report husband-wife collaboration in decision making.

2. Students see intrafamily relations as more distant and less congenial than parents indicate. This is especially true of student-parent relations.

3. Students more often report disagreements between themselves and their parents.

This situation is portrayed graphically in figure 5.1, which shows aggregate student and parent responses for ten items.[9] For all but one of the questions the graph shows the percentage of each sample giving what we judged to be the more favorable response.[10] On all but one item the parents gave the favorable response more frequently than students. The one reversal is for the item on which two separate questions were utilized and may be due to that fact. As noted, however, the differences are not large, being only three or four percentage points for several variables.

Several comparisons that do not fit the mold of figure 5.1 also

9. Excluded is the question about student-parent relations now compared to 3 years ago. It is hard to tell if one response is more favorable than another. The "better" and "worse" responses both indicate that a student and parent did not get along well at one time or another. A response of "about the same" can mean continuously good or bad relations.

10. Although most questions used in figure 5.1 had 3 response categories, typically one response was seldom given. In other cases, one response was more favorable than both others. Hence giving the percentage for only one response is justified.

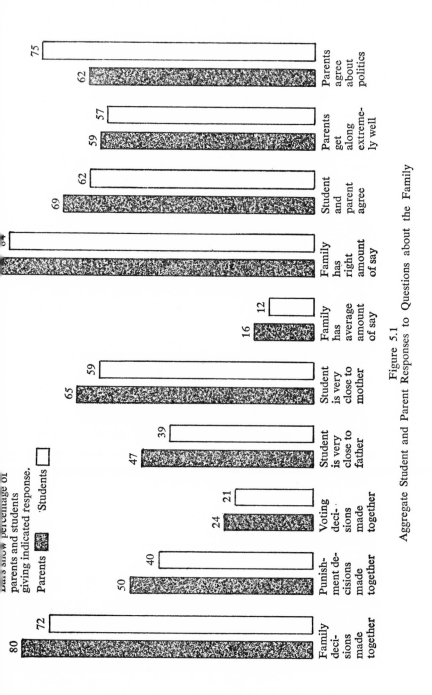

Bars show percentage of
parents and students
giving indicated response.

□ Students
▨ Parents

Figure 5.1

Aggregate Student and Parent Responses to Questions about the Family

Family decisions made together — 80 / 72

Punishment decisions made together — 50 / 40

Voting decisions made together — 24 / 21

Student is very close to father — 47 / 39

Student is very close to mother — 65 / 59

Family has average amount of say — 16 / 12

Family has right amount of say — 6̲4̲

Student and parent agree — 69 / 62

Parents get along extremely well — 59 / 57

Parents agree about politics — 62 / 75

show similar broad outlines together with some discrepancies worth noting. For example, the perceived role of fathers and mothers in family decision making shows a small difference. Mother dominance is reported with about equal frequency by both parents (7 percent) and offspring (9 percent). But separate or joint decision making is slightly more often reported by parents than students (83 percent versus 76 percent), while students more often report that the father is the boss (15 percent versus 10 percent). Reports of decision making in regard to punishment show similar but slightly larger differences.

The greatest discrepancy in student and parent reports concerns the path of compatabilities over the past several years. Seventy percent of the parents report a stable relationship with their teenage son or daughter; they "get along with" their child about the same as they did three years earlier. In contrast, only 51 percent of the students viewed relations with their parents as unchanging.[11] Apparently, arguments and disagreements that parents consider normal teenage behavior are not taken so lightly by teenagers themselves. Parents, using their longer experience and their own teenage days for comparison, no doubt expect some problems with their teenage children and handle them without much ado. Among teenagers, the problems and frustrations of growing into adulthood are more often viewed as the result of "old-fashioned" parents or parents who "won't let you do what you want." Thus students more frequently than parents report a period of conflict between older and younger generations.

That parents take teenage problems in stride to a greater extent than the students is supported by explanations of changes that did occur in student-parent feelings. When improved relations were reported at the time of the interview, parents were almost unanimous in attributing the improvement to maturation by the student. Ninety-four percent of the parents who reported improvement said that they now get along better with their child because he had "grown up," "gotten through the problem stage," "used to think he knew everything," and so on. A large majority

11. Of those reporting any change in their relationship, 57% of the parents and 62% of the students saw an improvement.

of students, 84 percent, likewise cited maturation as the reason for less tension, but they also cited with some frequency more specific problems that had been overcome, such as poor study habits, the need to use the family car, and problems in the family unit itself, such as a death or divorce. Where relations with parents have taken a turn for the worse, 83 percent of the parents and 67 percent of the students cite the obverse side of maturation —e.g., "he doesn't mind well now" or "you could reason with him then." Students again refer to specific activities (working, dating, drinking) or family problems considerably more often than do the parents. Students, then, provide a somewhat more turbulent picture of teenagers' relations with their parents and more often list specific causes rather than attributing fluctuations to the larger problem of achieving adult status.

I observed above that more students than parents cited some kind of current major disagreement. Do students report different kinds of disagreements as well? By and large the answer is no. Figure 5.2 shows the proportions of each sample reporting various types of conflicts (based on those reporting any disagreement). The overall similarity in the subjects reported is surprising when the nature of these disagreements is considered. Nearly as many parents as students reported some conflict involving the social life and activities of the youths. This includes all aspects of dating —frequency, hours, use of the car, choice of friends, etc. Similarly, almost as many students as parents reported disagreements concerning home life and personal habits—allowance, personal appearance, chores, and so on. In the aggregate, at least, parents are well aware of the students' concerns and desires about their social lives, and students are equally aware of parental desires concerning their home life and personal development.

Interestingly, the category showing the largest difference is that of social and political issues. Among the parents barely 6 percent reported any disagreements of this nature, while 20 percent of the students mentioned such conflicts. Some of the disagreements reported by students concerned the civil rights struggle, which was salient because the interviews were taken at the height of the civil rights movement. Equally many, however, dealt with politics in general or with a variety of specific issues.

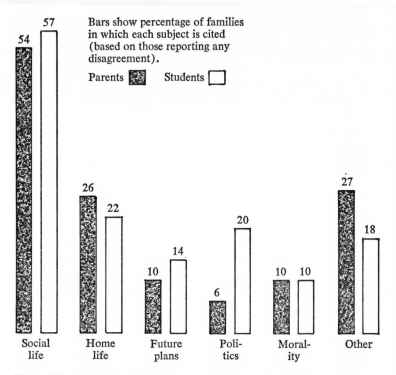

Figure 5.2
Subjects of Disagreement
between Students and Parents

NOTE: The percentages for each sample total more than 100% because multiple reasons were given.

The smaller proportion of parents reporting conflicts about social and political issues is probably symptomatic of a general unawareness among parents of the developing political attitudes of their offspring, a point already developed.

The aggregate responses of parents and students have revealed quite similar views of family life. Parents' reports were found to be consistently more favorable, but the differences were not large. In some ways this is remarkable, when one considers the variety of factors that might lead to generational differences. (These reasons will be discussed below.) Let us reserve any comments about the implications of the findings until the responses of student-parent pairs have been examined. Any illusion that the aggregate similarities are grounded in agreement among members of the same family will quickly be dispelled.

INDIVIDUAL COMPARISONS

Comparing descriptions of the family provided by student-parent pairs makes inescapable the conclusion that generic characteristics of the family, identifiable to parents and children alike, are not to be found. Figure 5.3 presents the correlations

.33	How well parents get along
.29	Student-mother closeness
.28	Student-father closeness
.25	How decisions on punishments are made
.22	How family decisions are made
.17	How decisions on voting are made How much say family has in child's affairs
.15	Whether students and parents disagree
.14	Listen to radio with family
.13	Whether parents agree on politics
.12	How students and parents get along
.08	Whether family has right amount of say in child's affairs Watch television with family

Figure 5.3
Tau-*b* Correlations between Student and Parent
Reports of Family Structure and Interaction

between parent and student responses for thirteen items. It is to be expected, of course, that these correlations would be somewhat below those for reports of political characteristics and especially demographic data. But it is surprising to see just how low the correlations are. Even the highest figure indicates considerable disagreement between parents and students, while those on the lower end indicate that their reports are very nearly independent.

What these correlations mean in terms of classifying families can be seen by the cross tabulation of parent and student responses. This is done in table 5.1 for two variables, one with a

Table 5.1
Student and Parent Responses to Two Items about Family Relationships
(In percentages)

Student's Response	Parent's Response			
	Extremely well	*About average*	*Not so well*	
Mother and father get along				*Total*
Extremely well	42	15	*	57
About average	17	21	1	39
Not so well	1	2	1	4
Total	60	38	2	100
				N = 1,599[a]
How much family has to say about student's activities	*A lot to say*	*About average*	*Left on own*	*Total*
A lot to say	21	5	14	40
About average	4	3	5	12
Left on own	15	8	25	48
Total	40	16	44	100
				N = 1,875

* Less than 1 percent.
[a] The number of cases for the upper portion of the table is reduced by the elimination of students with only one parent.

relatively high and the other with a low correlation. As noted earlier, the marginal totals for both samples are very similar. For the question of parental harmony, 64 percent of the families are rated similarly by parents and students. Almost all of the others differ by only one category, although this is largely an artifact of the dichotomous nature of the responses. When we judge the degree of intrusion by parents into students' actions, half of the families were similarly placed, while about a fifth were rated just a step apart. More than a quarter of the families were placed at opposite extremes by different family members. For both variables, agreement is much less than expected if we consider the family as a unit, viewed similarly by all members.

The order of the items by the size of the correlations is only partially explicable. Among the lowest correlations are the items inquiring about media attention in the family. Responses to these items are understandably poorly correlated since the referent in the question was not entirely clear. A student may have watched television with his father or with his brothers and sisters while his mother watched television mostly when the rest of the family was absent. If the student and his mother are paired, both could give valid but different responses. Other examples can easily be imagined. In fact, it is questionable whether these items should even be considered as tapping a single family characteristic from two different family members. I have included it here, however, to reinforce a point made in earlier chapters. If questions are not sufficiently precise and detailed, information is less valid or entirely lost. This point is well understood in general, but it is often overlooked when questions concern persons other than the respondent. My point is that it is particularly important in this case, for we are compounding other sources of error such as a lack of information.

Questions dealing with the parents alone tend to yield the highest correlations. The question about parental harmony and those on family decision making involve the students not at all or only as objects of parents' decisions. In contrast, questions involving both students and parents yielded somewhat lower correlations. In both cases, however, there are nagging exceptions. The assessment of parental political agreement, a parent-only item, has one of the lowest correlations, while the judgment of parent-student closeness shows comparatively high agreement. In the latter case, the fact that the questions distinguished between the mother and the father may have helped raise the correlation.

So far as we can tell, correlations are not improved noticeably by combining items. Some increment might have been expected due to the cancellation of minor differences on individual items.

To test this, a "decision index" was contrived from the questions about family decisions and decisions on the punishment of children.[12] This procedure did improve the distribution of responses by decreasing the bulge of respondents saying decisions were made separately or together. But the agreement between reports of the two generations is almost unchanged. The correlation for the combined items is .28, compared to .25 and .22 for the individual components. A similar combination of items was made for the questions about listening to radio and television by oneself or with the family. In this case the parent-student correlation for the combined items was slightly lower than for one of the individual questions. It may be that if one could collect a half-dozen or so items about each aspect of family living and combine them by a scaling procedure, the result would be higher correlations between student and parent reports. It is clear, however, that simple operations like those used here do not substantially alter the generally low correspondence between student and parent responses.

Responses to the open-ended question about the subjects of student-parent disagreements cannot be expressed in correlational terms, but they show that students and parents do not agree even about their disagreements. Since in many cases a student (or parent) cited some disagreement but his parent (child) did not mention any disagreement at all, overall student-parent consensus is low. Moreover, fine coding categories were used, so that student and parent responses often differ by shades of meaning. Rather than "loading the dice" against consensus, however, we asked a much less demanding question: among those student-parent pairs in which both members cited some major disagreement, how often does the disagreement fall into the same broad category, where the categories are those used earlier in the aggregate comparisons? It turns out that in only about half of these pairs is the same general type of disagreement cited. When the student and parent both say they disagree, as often as not they have different topics in mind. Once again, then, the aggregate similarity masks a rather tenuous correspondence between the responses of students and parents.

The disagreements between students and parents demonstrate

12. The index was similar to that illustrated in n. 14, chap. 2.

conclusively that "family structure," "family relationships," and "family agreement" are not single undifferentiated entities but that perceptions of the family differ considerably from one member to another. The fact that all the parent-student correlations are nonnegative and different from zero indicates that to a certain extent the reports of both generations are interdependent, presumably linked through the members' mutual experience in the family. But these mutual experiences are richly permeated with the individual interpretation of each family member.

An objection might be raised at this point that the questions used in this study lack specificity and require the respondent to make summary judgments about family structure and interaction. It may be argued that detailed, specific questions (e.g., *Who decides which television programs to watch when you and your spouse disagree?*) would have yielded greater intrafamily consensus. I personally doubt that much greater agreement would be found for more specific questions covering the same general topics. However, this is a point at which further validation efforts are worthwhile.[13] In any case, the questions used here are similar to those used in many studies of political socialization as well as child development studies in general. It is therefore important to know whether these questions yield valid data and if not, where (in addition to the possibility of the question form) the sources of error lie.[14]

A number of specific reasons can be cited for the varying inter-

13. Hess and Torney (1963) used some fairly specific questions in addition to general ones. They make no mention of different levels of agreement for these two types of questions. Although it is impossible to tell exact levels of agreement from their presentation, they do cite one rather specific question as revealing considerable disagreement between husbands and wives (p. 9).

14. With the findings of the present analysis in hand, it may be appropriate to ask whether other types of questions give more valid results and still satisfy the requirements of survey designs. It must be remembered that in many survey studies of political socialization, the family plays an important but limited role. Thus there is a premium on the amount of time and space devoted to any one topic. From this point of view, a few summary questions are preferable to a longer series of detailed questions. Also it is desirable to have questions that can be used for respondents of all ages, from young children to adults. With specific questions there may be a greater problem of making them appropriate for and understandable by all age groups.

pretations of the same family. One of the most obvious is simply that all family members do not observe the same aspects of family living. This explanation is given by Hess and Torney (1963) for one of their findings. Having noted (in contrast to this analysis) that the children in their sample named the mother as the "boss" more often than the parents did, they suggest that "children's tendency to give this response may reflect greater experience with the mother's decision-making powers in the home" (p. 12). This reason is especially persuasive when considering items that do not directly involve the student. Parents may base their evaluations on husband-wife interaction of which the child has little awareness. For example, arguments and disagreements may be harbored from children's eyes in order to avoid involving the children in parental squabbles. Decisions may be thrashed out and presented to youths in a united fashion, perhaps to prevent children from playing one parent against the other. Actions such as these, while not entering into the judgments of the students, could be the basis for parents' self-reports. Note that divergences due to viewing different family actions would not necessarily create generational cleavages of the type described earlier. In the example just given, decision making of which the student is unaware might find either the mother or the father more dominant than otherwise. Although the direction of the differences is thus unclear, experience with varying aspects of family living probably accounts for some of the disagreement between parents' and students' descriptions.

A second reason for discrepant accounts of the family is the use of different criteria for judging interaction which is observed. Kohn and Carroll (1960) cite evidence of different criteria in explaining disagreements in the reported relationship between working-class sons and their fathers. They suggest that for the parents the father's role in "setting limits" or establishing authority was a prime determinant of whether the child turned to his father. The children, however,

> could hardly be expected to share this evaluation of limit-setting. . . . The son is more likely to feel that he can turn to his father as readily as to his mother if the father does not play as large a part in setting limits for him as the mother does. This

is why working-class sons assess their relationships with their fathers so very differently from their parents (p. 382).

Their data support this reasoning. Of twenty-five working-class families in which the mother, father, and a fifth grade son were interviewed, there were five in which the parents said the child turns to the father as readily as the mother, but the son disputed this. In four of these families the father indicated that he plays a major role in setting limits. In another five families, the child said he turns to his father, but the parents disagreed. In four of these families, the father said that he does not have much to do with limit setting. As this example demonstrates, the differences resulting from the use of alternative criteria may be crosscutting rather than generational. Some students will apparently report better family relationships than parents, while in other families parents will give more favorable reports.

A closely related reason for divergent parent-student views is the use of different reference groups for rating family characteristics. For example, students may judge their own families on what they know or think they know about their friends' families. Parents may rate their relationships with their own children partly by comparison with other parents' experiences. Both parents and students may compare the current situation with what they think of as an ideal family. Another possibility is that parents' reports are somewhat affected by how they remember their parents and families when they were youths. This possibility will be examined in the section on bias below.

Generational differences in reporting about certain aspects of the parent-student relationship are suggested by a fourth reason for divergent responses from the two samples. The elemental fact that a student was usually asked about his parents (collectively) while a parent was asked only about himself and one particular child may account for some of the disagreement. When a parent is asked to describe his relationship with his child, the other parent need not be involved at all. A father can tell whether he and his son disagree regardless of any disagreements between the mother and son. If the spouse is brought into the picture, it will be only implicitly. For example, a mother who says she and her daughter get along very well may mean that they get along moderately well, but compared to the daughter-father relationship they are very compatible. But this sort of comparison is probably not likely when the questions exclude any mention of the spouse. For the students, by comparison, several questions were phrased in terms of "your family" or "your parents" rather than inquiring about the mother and father separately. In answering these questions, students who would otherwise distinguish between mother and father have to somehow "average" their feelings about each parent into a single response. If a student is then paired with his mother and father separately, it should not be surprising if his response differs slightly from that of one or both parents.

If this reasoning is correct, a somewhat higher rate of student-parent agreement should occur when the student question distinguishes between mother and father. This in fact happened in the one instance in which a distinction between the parents was made. The correlations expressing mother-student and father-student closeness were higher than for any other measure of the parent-student relationship.

One other piece of evidence, discovered accidentally, also supports the idea that generational differences are partially due to the failure to distinguish between the mother and father. When students were asked to describe the nature of any disagreements between themselves and their parents, a number of them volunteered that the disagreement was really with one parent. Responses were qualified by remarks such as, "My father and I don't agree on . . . ," "my mother thinks that . . . ," "my father agrees with me but my mother. . . ." Other students indicated that the disagreement was with both parents, with the remainder giving no indication. Of those who could have distinguished between the parents (i.e., a disagreement was indicated and more than one parent was present in the home), 18 percent did so, while a quarter more indicated that the dispute involved both parents.

The information about which parent was involved in the dispute can be used to make the reports of a student and one parent more comparable. Reports by students of disagreements with a parent not interviewed can reasonably be excluded from the student-parent comparison on the grounds that the parent would probably not mention disputes involving his or her spouse only. Since many students had no major disagreement with either parent or lived with one parent, the distinction between mother and father does not greatly affect the estimated disagreement rate in the entire sample. Initially 38 percent of the students reported a disagreement with their parents. Excluding student reports of disagreements with a parent not interviewed lowers this proportion to 35 percent. While this is only a small reduction, it does bring the proportion of students citing a disagreement closer to the proportion of parents (31 percent) who noted some dispute. Moreover, had students been asked explicitly which parent they disagreed with, or had the distinction between mother and father involved all students rather than just those reporting disagreements, the effect might have been much larger.[15] At any rate, the role of each parent in stimulating children's responses about the family deserves further investigation.

Another reason for the differences between student and parent reports is the lack of communication between parents and offspring concerning family interaction. In contrast to demographic and political variables, family structure and relationships are unlikely to be the subject of repeated conversations (or other reinforcing devices such as filling out forms that ask for the father's occupation). At times these topics force themselves into discussions, as when parents sharply and vocally disagree with their children's actions or when the student is so upset with his parents that he openly displays his emotions. Usually, however, family interaction is not the focus of attention. And even when it is, there are certain inhibitions to the free flow of ideas. One does not often tell his parents that they do not get along very well or tell his father that the mother makes most of the decisions. Thus students and parents seldom check their perceptions with each other. Since their disagreements are not identified, they cannot be consciously resolved. Under these conditions, differences in perceptions are likely to remain and proliferate.

15. On the other hand, contrary evidence is found in that the correlations between student and parent reports are no higher for one-parent than for two-parent families.

Bias in Students' and Parents' Responses

A final explanation for the differences between student and parent reports is the existence of several kinds of bias that differentially affect responses of the two generations. We first return to the problem of bias toward socially acceptable responses. It has already been observed that parents on the whole gave slightly more favorable responses than students. Here the individual basis for this pattern can be seen.[16]

By matching students and parents as before, we can observe for each pair whether the response of one member is more favorable than that of the other member. The procedure can be illustrated using table 5.1, presented earlier. For the question on how well the parents get along with each other, 64 percent of the student-parent pairs gave identical answers. Of the pairs not giving similar responses, those above the diagonal (16 percent) represent cases in which the students' response depicts a more acceptable family situation. For example, the student says his parents get along extremely well, while his parents say they get along about average or, in a few cases, not so well. The 20 percent of the cases below the diagonal are pairs in which the parent's response is more favorable. In the second example, we assume that the middle response, "about average," is somewhat more acceptable than either more or less attempted intervention by the parent in the student's affairs. Students, but not parents, give the average response in 9 percent of the pairs, while in 13 percent of the pairs the parent says "average" but the student disagrees.[17]

16. From a technical point of view, I cannot really show that bias exists by using the present data. A demonstration of bias presumes the existence of some standard against which to lay the observations in order to observe the amount and direction of distortion. I have pointed out, however, that neither students' nor parents' responses can be accepted as a standard. Strictly speaking, then, the existence of response bias cannot be proved or disproved here. What can be observed is that reports of one generation differ systematically from those of the other generation. So long as it is clear that this is what we are observing, use of the term "bias" should not be misleading.

17. As this example demonstrates, on some questions students and parents may give equally unfavorable answers.

Applying the foregoing procedure to each of the variables used above generates the series of comparisons in figure 5.4. For each variable the shaded bar shows the percentage of parents giving more favorable responses than their children and the unshaded bar shows the percentage of students giving more favorable responses than their parents. For all but one question parents gave socially acceptable responses more often than students. The exception finds students frequently saying the parents agree on political matters while the parents find something about which they disagree. (This reversal may be an artifact of the use of different student and parent questions.) Some of the discrepancies between students' and parents' descriptions of the family can thus be attributed to a tendency on the part of parents to give more favorable responses than students. Not that parents have a monopoly on acceptable answers. In many pairs the student's response is more favorable than the parent's. In fact, the bias introduced by the inflation of good qualities by parents is not very large.

I do not attribute the slight bias in parents' responses primarily to a conscious desire to appear more acceptable to others, although undoubtedly this motive is important to a few respondents. Does the bias then indicate that parents are more susceptible to the feelings of others and that they unconsciously try to present a more favorable self-image? Not necessarily. I have indicated repeatedly that parents probably interpret family behavior differently from teenagers, taking a long-range view of everyday conflicts and problems. Students' responses, I suggested, are influenced more by a recurrent series of minor crises that in retrospect appear almost trivial. If this is true, parents should be expected to give more favorable pictures of family living. On the other hand, the fact that only a small amount of bias is observed in parents' responses suggests that this explanation of student-parent differences has limited usefulness. Thus, the more important conclusion to be derived from this analysis is that bias in socially desirable directions creates fewer student-parent differences than previously supposed. While the differences are in the direction predicted by the studies cited earlier, they pose a much less serious threat to family descriptions than originally suspected.

Another potential source of bias is that a student's report about

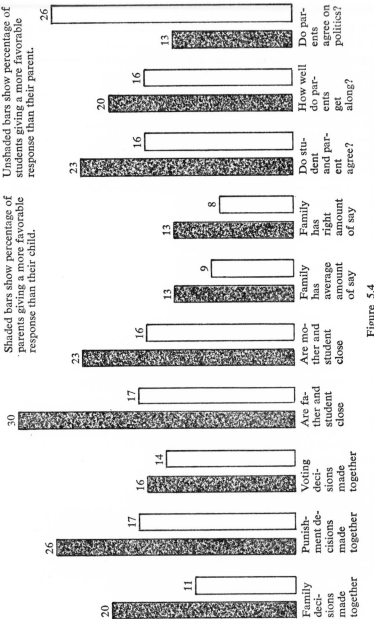

Shaded bars show percentage of parents giving a more favorable response than their child.

Unshaded bars show percentage of students giving a more favorable response than their parent.

Figure 5.4

Percentage of Parents and Students Giving More Favorable Responses on Family Relationships one parent may be distorted by his perception of the other parent. Though the concern is quite general, we are limited here to the topic of parent-student closeness because it is the only one on which students were asked about the mother and father separately. Using the measure of bias described in the appendix with these data, we find that 61 percent of the students' reports are biased toward their perceived relationship with the other parent. Clearly this is not a large amount of bias and we cannot attribute most student-parent differences to the tendency of students to bias their responses in this respect. On the other hand, enough bias is present to affect family descriptions. Let us ask, for example, how similar are the mother-student and father-student relationships. Using parents' reports, we find a correlation of .23 between the closeness of a student to his mother and to his father. Students' reports of the same relationship yield a correlation of .31, indicating a somewhat greater consistency in a student's relations with his parents.[18] Thus, using a single source of information increases the apparent consistency in multiple relationships. That this tendency to inflate consistency is not limited to students will be confirmed as we examine an analogous type of bias in parents' reports.

The last type of bias to be considered here is whether parents' responses are biased toward the perceived atmosphere of their own families. Parents were asked about general decision making and about decisions concerning the punishment of children in the family in which they grew up. They were also asked how close they felt, as teenagers, to their mother and their father. For these items we can perform the same type of operation just used in searching for bias in students' responses.

For each of the variables, nearly the same amount of bias is found in parents' responses. When students and parents disagreed about the current division of power between the husband and wife, 66 percent and 64 percent of the parents' reports about general decision making and child discipline, respectively, were biased toward the perceived division of power in the parents'

18. Both of these correlations are based on the 430 families in which both mother and father were interviewed.

adolescent family. In the case of the parent-child relationship, the situation is more complicated. The student-father or student-mother relationship can be used. In either case, we can look for bias toward the parent's reported relationship with the parent of the same sex or the opposite sex. In any event, the results are similar for all of these comparisons. When a student disagrees with his father about how close they are, 62 percent of the time the latter's report is in the direction of the reported relationship with his own father; 67 percent of the time it is in the direction of the reported relationship with his mother. Where the student and mother disagree, the mother's report is closer to her perceived relationship with her father and mother 62 percent and 60 percent of the time, respectively.

These measures of bias are of a magnitude similar to that found in students' reports of their relationship with each parent. That is, while the amount of bias is not too great, it is large enough to affect some descriptive matters. Consider the question of intergenerational change: How similar are the families in which the students are growing up and the families in which their parents grew up? The answer is that it depends on who the reports come from; more specifically, if the reports come from a single respondent rather than two respondents, the observed similarity will be significantly greater. For comparing characteristics of families across generations, several different sources of information are potentially available. However, since the students' grandparents were not interviewed, information about the older generation family has to come from the parents. Information about the younger generation family can come from the parents or the students.

Table 5.2 shows the correlations between descriptions of the two families using alternative reports about the student's family. When the parent is the only source of information, there are moderate relationships between the two generations on the locus of power and parent-child closeness. These relationships nearly vanish when students' reports of the current generation are utilized. The substantive conclusion about the similarity of family characteristics in two generations, like the observed similarity of

Table 5.2
Similarity of Reports about Parent's and Student's Families
Using One versus Two Sources of Information

| | Source of information about | | |
Topic	Parent's Family (as an adolescent)	Student's Family	Tau-b Correlation between Reports about the Two Families
Family decision	Parent	Parent	.08
making	Parent	Student	.01
Decisions about	Parent	Parent	.17
punishment	Parent	Student	.04
Closeness of father and child (in both families)	Parent	Parent	.19
	Parent	Student	.07
Closeness of mother and child (in both families)	Parent	Parent	.19
	Parent	Student	.09
Closeness of father and student and father and his mother	Parent	Parent	.25
	Parent	Student	.08
Closeness of mother and student and mother and her father	Parent	Parent	.21
	Parent	Student	.08

student-mother and student-father closeness, thus depends on the use of one or multiple sources of information.

More generally, the figures in table 5.2 can be compared fruitfully with those in table 3.6. Although the variables are quite different in the two cases, they both show that the use of one source of information to characterize distinguishable objects (individuals, families, relationships) increases the apparent similarity of those objects. The comparison also suggests that there is a rough correspondence between the agreement of the two sources on the objects they jointly characterize and the degree to which similarity is overestimated. The items represented in table 5.2 show about the same level of agreement as the political interest item, and with one exception (family decision making) these variables revealed the greatest exaggeration of similarity. The features most accurately perceived were much less affected. Students barely overestimated parental similarity regarding the presidential vote and actually underestimated the similarity of the mothers' and fathers' education (chapter 2).

Correlates of Student-Parent Agreement

Comparisons of students' reports with those of their parents revealed a considerable amount of disagreement in descriptions of family characteristics. Although variations in the amount of agreement among subgroups of the population will not alter this basic conclusion, it is important to examine these variations for at least two reasons. First, differing agreement rates may affect the evaluation of data from samples or subsamples of selected population strata. If student-parent agreement is significantly higher within certain types of families, this should be considered in evaluating data collected from these families. Since socialization studies often use samples purposively limited to certain types of families (e.g., only nuclear families, those with an only child, etc.), different studies may be based on data that vary widely in rates of intrafamily agreement. In a heterogeneous sample, the use of control categories can have the same effect.

A second reason for seeking correlates of student-parent agreement is for whatever insight it may provide about the interpretation and explanation of discrepancies in student and parent reports. To the extent that variations in agreement rates depend on structural and demographic features of the family, these features can suggest conditions that promote agreement among family members or contribute to divergent views. Ways of gathering data that are more often agreed upon might be a direct result. On the other hand, if agreement rates are unrelated to sociological features of the family, we can conclude only that individual psychological traits or idiosyncratic factors account for a large part of the variance in the descriptions given by individual family members. The task of collecting common views of the family would then prove very difficult, if not impossible.

One of the most obvious places to begin is with student-parent sex combinations. Is agreement persistently greater among students and their mothers because of more frequent interaction with the mother? Do students agree with the parent of the same sex more often than the other parent? To answer these questions we computed the correlations between reports from sons and fathers, sons and mothers, daughters and fathers, and daughters and mothers for each of the variables used above. In the degree that these correlations show any pattern, daughters and mothers tend to have the highest rates of agreement while sons and mothers reveal the least agreement. The daughter-mother combination yields the highest correlation for over half of the variables and never shows the lowest coefficient; sons and mothers have the lowest correlation a little less than half the time and never have the highest rate of agreement. But the differences are not large, the mean difference between the highest and lowest correlation for each variable being only .12. Further evidence of the mild differences in agreement rates is found in the average correlations: daughters and mothers .24, daughters and fathers .19, sons and fathers .18, sons and mothers .16. The observed amount of agreement, then, depends only to a limited degree on the sex of respondents.

A second obvious categorization of families is by the presence of both, only one, or neither of the natural parents in the household. This is an important variable because changes in family composition can have an enormous effect on all aspects of family interaction, especially student-parent relationships. And we previously noted the effects of family composition on reports of demographic data. However, in this case no consistent differences emerged for the two-parent, one-parent, or surrogate-parent cases. This was true on the items concerning the parents alone and those dealing with student-parent interaction. The highest rate of agreement occurred with about equal frequency in each of the three types of families, and the average correlations were very similar.

Other characteristics of the parents and family affect agreement rates only at the extremes or not at all. The age of the parents might reasonably be related to the level of student-parent agreement. As the distance between generations becomes greater, parents may less often interpret family interaction the same way the students do. Since the age distribution of the parents has little dispersion, parents were sorted into five different groups, with the oldest consisting of those 56 years or older. It turns out that only among the oldest parents is there a reduced amount of agreement with their children and then only among items concerning student-parent interaction. The number of children in the family, although plausibly related to agreement rates, shows no effect, even at the extremes. A slight tendency can be observed for families with low-status occupations to agree less frequently. This goes hand in hand with the somewhat lower rates of agreement among blacks. These differences, however, are quite small and not entirely consistent across the dependent variables. Agreement rates are unrelated to the level of education of the parents.

This analysis shows that while some variations in agreement rates can be found for subgroups of the population, the variations are typically small and inconsistent. Moreover, in no case did agreement dramatically improve so that anything approaching complete agreement was achieved. These facts indicate that samples or subsamples carefully chosen to represent certain types of families would find about the same generally low levels of agreement observed earlier for the total sample of students and parents. Equally important, we cannot account for variations in agreement rates on the basis of the types of characteristics utilized. Lack of agreement cannot be attributed except in a minimal way to the sex of the student or parent, the composition of the family, or its social status. Thus the problem of low agreement between parents and their children cannot be avoided by treating only special subgroups nor can it be explained away as simply the result of certain accidents of family composition.

The analysis in this chapter forces us to a basically negative conclusion about the validity of data about family structure and relationships among family members. The low level of agreement among students and parents—along with the inability to find correlates of agreement and the inability to locate correctable sources of error—seriously erodes our confidence in these questions as a means of tapping family features. Moreover, the aggregate similarity of the reports together with other findings suggests strongly that the differences between student and parent reports cannot be laid to generational cleavages. Nevertheless, before putting this question of generational differences to rest, we will want to compare husbands' and wives' reports in chapter 8. It is still possible that spouses will show widespread agreement where children and parents revealed very little. I will leave a discussion of the implications of the present findings until that point.

PART TWO

COMPARISON AND EVALUATION OF HUSBANDS' AND WIVES' REPORTS ABOUT THE FAMILY AND EACH OTHER

6: Demographic and Related Information about Spouses

At this point our attention shifts exclusively to the mothers and fathers of our sample students. As I mentioned in the introduction, there are many circumstances in which, and a number of reasons why, respondents are relied upon for information about their spouses. Yet there are no more studies of the accuracy of spouses' reports than of students' and parents' reports about each other. In this chapter we begin to fill this void by examining husbands' and wives' reports about each other's demographic and related characteristics. In addition to the subjects covered in chapter 2, we will consider a number of characteristics that are likely to be sought from spouses but not from children.

NATURE OF THE DATA

As in the parent-student case, we can most often assume that respondents give accurate accounts of their own characteristics. Thus, for example, we will assume that husbands give correct reports of their occupation, their military service, and their union membership, if any, and we will speak of the wife's accuracy in reporting these kinds of information. Husbands and wives will both be assumed to give truthful accounts of their own education and whether or not they have worked for the government, and we will gauge the accuracy of each spouse's knowledge about the other one. The same problems (of unique circumstances such as the "well-educated" high school dropout) and caveats (about interviewer and coding error) apply here as in the parent-student situation. As before, however, I regard these as minor in nature and partially testable through the accuracy of information on the number of children in the family.

There are, in addition, a number of variables for which we cannot automatically assume that one spouse's report is correct. Length of residence in the local community was the only example of this sort in the student-parent case. This example is repeated here but is joined by several others. These measures—home ownership, family and head of household income, length of marriage, and subjective social class—are in all but one instance (subjective class) characterized by an objectively correct answer. However, in the event of husband-wife disagreement it would take a heroic assumption to attribute accuracy to one partner and error to the other. While husbands may in fact be better accountants of the family's income and of home ownership, and while wives may more often recall correctly the length of their marriage, I am unwilling to attribute credit and blame for discrepancies in these reports.[1] The case of subjective social class is somewhat different, since it is by definition not an objective feature of the household. I expect a high level of husband-wife agreement on this measure—and include it here because it is often used in the same way as more objective measures— but it is obviously appropriate in this case to speak of agreement rather than accuracy of spouses' reports.

Questions Used in This Study

Several of the questions used here have already been introduced in chapter 2. As noted there, the husband (father) was asked one or more questions in order to produce a specific description of his occupation. Coding was done with a detailed census classification of 500 occupations, the Duncan decile code, the less elaborate SRC code, and the SRC industry code. We will also utilize information about the respondent's employment status (employed, unemployed, or retired) and whether the husband worked for himself, someone else, or both. As noted in chapter 2, this auxiliary information was gathered from parents but not from children. Wives were asked parallel questions about themselves and their husbands using identical questions except, of course, for the referent. Their

1. For one thing, it is known that respondents of both sexes make errors, sometimes of considerable magnitude, in reporting economic information. See Lansing et al. (1961) and Ferber (1966).

responses were coded in the same way as the males' answers. Husbands were not asked about their wives' employment (no doubt due to male chauvinism).

Reports of education were also discussed earlier. I need add only two points here. First, we can now check on several aspects of education—specific college(s) attended, college major, degrees received, and types of noncollege training—as well as just the overall amount of education. Second, each parent was asked about himself (herself) and his or her spouse. This allows us to check the accuracy of both husbands' and wives' perceptions. Two other items, the number of children in the family and the length of residence in the local community, are also carried over from the student-parent analysis.

In addition to these reports, there are a number of items of information that were not used in the student-parent comparisons. Several of these formed a series about past and present employment. First, males were asked if they had ever served in the military; wives were asked about their husbands:

> *Have you (Has your husband) ever served in the United States Armed Forces—that is in the Army, Navy, Air Force, or other branch?* (If yes) *During what years was that?*

Nonmilitary governmental work was also inquired about. Note that the question asks about the respondent and his or her spouse:

> *Aside from military service, have you or your (spouse) ever worked as a* civilian *for the federal, a state, or a local government?* (If yes) *What government agency or department was that?* (Be sure federal, state, or local is indicated.) *During what years was that?*

Responses were coded so that we can analyze several facets of possible employment, e.g., the time period, the level of government, and length of employment.

Next, an inquiry was made about union membership:

> *Does anyone in this household belong to a labor union?* (If yes) *Who is it that belongs? What union is that? About how long have you (has he) belonged to this union?*

Here, too, we can consider several parts of the response—who be-longs to a union, the specific union, and the length of membership.

Finally, near the end of the interview, respondents were asked for their subjective social class placement:

> *There is quite a bit of talk these days about different social classes. Most people say they belong either to the middle class or to the working class. Do you ever think of yourself as being in one of these classes?* (If yes) *Which one?* (If no) *Well, if you had to make a choice, would you call yourself* middle-*class or* working-*class?*

Provision was made in the coding for the small number of individuals who call themselves upper- or lower-class or who refuse to accept the idea of classes.

Economic facts were sought in a straightforward fashion. Home ownership was established by asking: *Do you own your own home here, or rent, or what?* Family income and head of the household's income were determined by handing the respondent a card with numbered categories. The individual had only to give the number of the category into which the desired income fell.[2]

The final new item in this chapter was simply phrased: *How long have you been married?* It followed, of course, a question on marital status and was asked only of those currently married and living with their spouses.

INDIVIDUAL COMPARISONS

Husbands and wives as unfailingly as students are able to provide the desired information about each other. Even though we asked parents more detailed information about each other, such as college majors and the particular years the husband served in the armed forces, "don't know" responses are typically 1 percent or less. The only exception to this is in regard to income, and even here only 3.7 percent of the wives said they did not know the anticipated family income.

In the aggregate, husbands' and wives' responses are very similar.

2. The categories were: 0. Under $1,000; 1. $1,000–1,999; 2. $2,000–2,999; 3. $3,000–3,999; 4. $4,000–4,999; 5. $5,000–5,999; 6. $6,000–7,499; 7. $7,500–9,999; 8. $10,000–14,999; 9. $15,000 or over.

Most important, however, are two further points. First, there is no systematic bias apparent in the overall responses. Women, for example, report high family incomes slightly less often by putting 5 percent fewer of the families in the $10,000-and-over bracket. In terms of social class, on the other hand, the small difference goes in the opposite direction with wives putting 6 percent more of the families in the middle class than the working class. The second important point is that with only one exception there is every indication that responses would be accurate in the aggregate for other types of samples. Unlike students' and parents' reports about each other's partisanship, the evidence to be presented below on inter-category variations in accuracy suggests that aggregate responses will be highly accurate for almost all types of samples. The single exception concerns whether or not the respondent worked for the government. In the present sample both husbands and wives under-estimated the proportion of spouses working for the government by close to 10 percent, and the error could clearly be greater for some samples. This will be taken up again in the section on intercategory variations in accuracy.

The degree of accuracy of most of the information is conveniently summarized by the correlations given in figure 6.1. Two salient features are immediately obvious. First, in every comparison that can be made, spouses' reports are more accurate than children's (fig. 2.1). Second, insofar as we can tell, husbands' and wives' reports appear to be about equally accurate. The primary example of this is in the two reports of education. In addition, however, reports of governmental employment by husbands and wives are about equally accurate. In several other cases in which there is no objective response, examination of the disagreements uncovers no evidence to suggest greater bias or error by either respondent. Thus while my evidence is conclusive only for education, I feel that husbands as well as wives can be relied upon for information about their spouses.

The order of the items in figure 6.1 requires little discussion. At the very top are factual items on which we expect and find almost complete accuracy and on which errors are probably attributable to interviewers, coders, and idiosyncratic circumstances. As with the students, education and occupation are both reported accurately,

.97	Own home or renting
.96	Number of children in family
.94	Length of marriage
.91	Husband's education (i.e., accuracy of wife's report)
.90	Number of years of husband's military service Some family member belongs to a labor union Husband works for himself, himself and someone else, or someone else
.89	Wife's education
.83	Anticipated family income Husband's occupation (SRC code)
.78	Husband's occupation (Duncan decile code)
.66	Length of residence in local community
.63	Husband has worked for a government at some time
.62	Wife has worked for a government at some time
.52	Subjective social class (middle or working)

Figure 6.1
Tau-*b* Correlations between Husbands' and Wives'
Reports of Demographic and Related Information

but with reports of education being slightly better. A noticeably lower correlation results for reports of length of residence in the local community.

Surveying the other items—those not included in the student-parent comparisons—we find several instances of high conjugal agreement. Not surprisingly, couples almost invariably agree on whether they own their home or are renting as well as how long they have been married. More significantly, there is widespread agreement on gross categorizations of length of military service,[3] union membership, and the family's income. In the latter case it should not be thought that there is complete agreement about family finances. Even though the responses were lumped into categories $1,000 or more in width, only 72 percent of the husbands and wives chose exactly the same category. However, the high correlation reflects the fact that widely discrepant views rarely occur.

Only two of the new measures, one pertaining to both the husband and wife, reveal markedly lower levels of agreement between spouses. The problem with determining governmental work apparently stems from a variety of minor complications. This matter will be dealt with in detail below, where some suggestions will be given for improving collection of these data. This leaves subjective social class as the only measure showing considerable disagreement and for which there is no apparent solution.[4] In percentage terms this correlation means that about a quarter of the husbands and wives differ in their perceived class position. By definition, of course, this is a subjective measure and we cannot say that respondents have given incorrect reports. On the other hand, it is typically felt that a husband and wife share a class position. This being so, it is reasonable to question the utility of a measure on which husband and wife disagree as often as they do here.[5] The arguments in favor of a

3. Responses were coded as follows: no military service, 0–2, 3–5, 6–9, 10 or more years. In retrospect, there is no reason why exact numbers of years could not have been coded.

4. A few respondents said "upper" or "lower" class or refused to accept the idea of classes. Before the correlation was computed, however, both the husband and wife were eliminated if either gave one of these responses.

5. Beck (forthcoming) finds quite low correlations between reports of subjective class across successive waves of panel studies in the United States and Great Britain. The pattern of correlations is such that unreliability rather than true change is suggested.

subjective rather than objective measure of social class sound convincing, and it is very probably the case that some families regard themselves and live in a manner more often associated with the other class than the one with which they would be grouped "objectively." But when husband and wife so often disagree on their relative position, I seriously doubt the utility of the measure. And while it is inappropriate to refer to response "error," it is still the case that relationships between subjective social class and other variables will be seriously attenuated by the ambiguous categorization of many individuals or families.

In addition to the information summarized in figure 6.1, auxiliary information was obtained from husbands and wives about some of the subjects. This additional information supports the conclusion that husbands and wives are accurate reporters of their spouse's demographic characteristics. For example, 93 percent of the husbands and wives gave similar reports about the period of time during which the husband served in the armed forces.[6] We also asked about the length and time of service, if any, as a government employee. With regard to both aspects some 89 percent of the husbands' reports and 78 percent of the wives' reports agreed with those of their spouses.[7]

Reports about union membership also called for specifying exactly which family members belonged to a union, which union they belonged to, and how long they had been union members. Insofar as we can tell, about 95 percent of the spouses agreed on who belonged to a union.[8] The specific union was also widely agreed

6. The categories were as follows: 1. Prior to 1919; 2. 1919–40; 3. 1941–46; 4. 1947–53; 5. 1954–65; 6. Combination of categories 2 and 3; 7. Combination of categories 3 and 4; 8. Other combinations.

7. These percentages are based on the following categories. For number of years: 0–1; 2–5; 6–9; 10–15; 20 or more. For time of employment: 1. Before 1933; 2. 1933–39; 3. 1940–46; 4. 1947–60; 5. 1961–65; 6. Combination of categories 3 and 4; 7. Combination of categories 4 and 5; 8. Other combinations.

8. There was an ambiguity in the code for this question that prevents me from making as exact a comparison as I would like. This problem in our own code again calls attention to the need to specify very clearly, in both question and the coding, that precise individual or individuals to whom the response applies because the husband and wife as well as any additional adults in the household are by no means identical.

upon. Limiting the cases to those in which only the husband belonged to a union (to avoid ambiguity about who belonged), we find that 82 percent of the spouses agreed on whether it was an AFL union, a CIO union, or an independent union. Even when the full list of over 200 unions is used, 79 percent of the husbands and wives gave identical responses. Finally, there was a correlation of .76 between spouses' reports of the length of union membership.

Educational attainment is another area in which we can assess the accuracy of auxiliary information. Two topics were considered. On the question of college majors, some loss of detail is encountered, especially in certain categories. This is spelled out more fully in the section on response accuracy within categories. Nonetheless, the gross outlines of fields of study are quite accurately portrayed by spouses. Thus if used carefully, information about college majors could be profitably gathered from husbands or wives. As we would expect, specific colleges are salient enough that most husbands and wives can provide accurate information about their spouses' attendance. Specifically, 89 percent of the husbands and 88 percent of the wives accurately indicated the specific college attended by his or her spouse.[9]

Bias in Husbands' and Wives' Responses

Given the high degree of accuracy of spouses' reports, biased reports are not likely to be a serious problem. Nevertheless, we need to consider briefly the possibility that responses are biased in socially acceptable directions.

Education and occupation are the two most likely candidates for such bias. Either spouse might improve the image of the other one by overestimating his or her education. The husband's occupation might be made to look a little higher status. In practice, spouses' reports, like those of the students', show no detectable upward bias. Whereas 5 percent of the husbands overestimate their wives' educational attainments, 9 percent give underestimates. Similarly, 7 percent of the wives exaggerate their husbands' education, but 10

9. This comparison was limited to those receiving a college degree. If all those who attended college are considered, the percentages drop to 79 and 84, respectively.

percent diminish it. In both instances, the underreporting comes in considerable measure from the failure to mention noncollege training. But even when these cases are excluded, underestimates are as frequent as overestimates. The same situation holds for occupation. Using the Duncan decile code, 10 percent of the wives' reports upgrade their husbands' status; but at the same time, 14 percent downgrade it. With the SRC classification, errors in each direction amount to 6 percent.

These results are, of course, affected by the distribution of respondents across the education and occupation measures, and it might be suspected that the greater frequency of underestimates is artifactual. For example, the sample contains considerably more husbands at the upper end of the occcupation ratings than at the lower end—in fact, 41 percent in the top two categories versus 8 percent in the bottom two. If some portion of the error were uniformly distributed in each category (say, by coding errors), the heavier weighting of high-status occupations would exaggerate underreports. This is so because overreports could hardly occur in the top categories and indeed could not occur at all in the highest category. This possibility was entertained by using the error in each category to give a rough estimate of the errors that would result with more uniform distributions of respondents for both education and occupation.[10] The results indicate, as they should, that the ratio of underestimates to overestimates decreases as the distribution becomes more rectangular. However, the conclusion remains that under most circumstances underexaggeration of spouses' status or achievements is at least as likely as overestimations. Social desirability response error does not pervade reports of education and occupation.

Perceptual bias should also be considered in two other cases, although here we cannot attribute error to either spouse. In the case of family income, wives tend to underestimate, or husbands to overestimate, the true state of affairs. Eighteen percent of the wives gave lower estimates of the family income than their husbands, while in 10 percent of the cases the husband gave the lower esti-

10. The results are rough because the number of cases is small in some categories so that estimates of errors must be taken lightly.

mate. As noted, the discrepancies were rarely large but did have the effect of slightly underestimating the proportion of families with high incomes. A contrasting picture of perceptual bias is given by self-perceptions of social class. On the basis of the income and occupation reports, women might be expected to see themselves as working-class more often than men. But in fact, when disagreements occurred, some 15 percent of the time the wife said middle-class and her husband said working-class. The opposite pattern occurred only 9 percent of the time.

These mildly conflicting results for income and subjective class bolster our confidence that response errors for demographic variables are not much affected by social desirability bias by either husbands or wives. If either sex were predisposed to upward exaggeration, we would expect a more consistent pattern. As it is, which spouse gives the more favorable reports depends on the question at hand, and replies from neither source are likely to be consistently altered toward more favorable responses.

As a final note on possible biases, we consider the possibility that families would look more homogeneous using one respondent to report about both husband and wife than using independent sources. This could be examined only for the case of education. As with the student reports, similarity of this family feature is not exaggerated by using only one respondent. The correlation between education of husband and wife is .54 using the individual reports of each spouse. If we use either the husband's or the wife's report of both spouses, the correlation drops slightly to .52. In addition, the relative education of husbands versus wives is nearly identically estimated using any of the reports.

Together with the high level of accuracy found in most instances, the failure to find any consistent bias in either husbands' or wives' responses supports the view that spouses' reports of demographic features can be used with confidence. We must, however, still consider the accuracy of reports given within each response category.

Accuracy of Spouses' Reports within Individual Categories

The accuracy of reports about spouses' education can be seen in table 6.1 for each level of education. For the most part the per-

Table 6.1
Accuracy of Husbands' and Wives' Reports of Spouse's Education

Spouse's Education (own report)	Husband's Education (as reported by wife)		Wife's Education (as reported by husband)	
	Percent accurate	*Number of cases*	*Percent accurate*	*Number of cases*
0–7 grades	87	51	94	31
8 grades	77	71	86	56
9–11 grades	83	85	84	92
12 grades	87	96	92	153
12 grades and noncollege school	60	53	65	72
Some college	91	82	96	57
Bachelor's degree	90	51	92	42
Advanced degree	80	32	63	12
Total	83	521	86	515

centages of accurate responses are high for both the husband's and
the wife's education. However, suggestions can be made for further
improvement in two areas. First, while spouses more often than
children correctly mention some noncollege schooling, it is obvious
that a good deal of this kind of training is not mentioned. To see
what type of schooling was being neglected, we examined the cases
in which the respondent mentioned some noncollege schooling. For
husbands, insofar as we can tell from the relatively small number
of cases, there is no particular pattern to the kind of schooling not
mentioned by wives. Correspondence courses, training in the armed
services, night-school courses, and so on all contribute a small portion of the error. For wives, on the other hand, business training is
clearly the culprit, accounting for about half of the cases in which
husbands failed to report noncollege training.

This situation might well be alleviated by including some examples when asking about noncollege training. In fact, this approach
should probably be used when asking about respondents and
spouses alike. Thus, for example, instead of simply asking respondents, "Have you had any other schooling?" two questions might be
asked. First, "Have you attended college?" Second, "Have you had
any other schooling, such as business courses, beauty school, correspondence courses, courses in the military service, and so on?"
Similar questions could be developed for spouses. While such questions might be unnecessarily detailed for some purposes, they would

seem essential if we wish to be certain of picking up information about noncollege schooling.[11]

The second possible point of improvement in educational reports concerns advanced degrees. When such degrees were held by wives, they were particularly underreported. While the number of cases in this category is small, we note a similar decline in accuracy among student reports. And while reports of advanced degrees among husbands are quite accurate, it seems anomalous that they are less accurately reported than the holding of bachelor's degrees. I strongly suspect that the problem here lies in the question rather than in spouse's faulty memories. The question asks about the degree(s) earned and requires the interviewer to phrase it so that multiple degrees are clearly called for, or it relies on the respondent's spontaneously mentioning multiple degrees. If accurate information is desired on this score, as it might well be with the increase in graduate education in recent years, questions should be explicitly designed with this feature in mind.

Although it is likely to be a less serious problem, I make this suggestion even if information is sought about the respondent himself or herself rather than about a spouse. In the "bachelor's degree" category, 3 percent of the 10 percent error in wives' reports is accounted for by the wife mentioning an advanced degree while the husband failed to mention such an achievement. Thus it would appear that respondents' self-reports slightly underestimate the attainment of advanced degrees. A specific question to clarify this matter surely seems called for.

Reports of spouses' college majors revealed more discrepancies than reports of overall education, and the errors were more highly concentrated. The level of accuracy will of course depend on how precise we wish to be. I have grouped the responses into seven broad categories.[12] The figures make it clear that health-related, en-

11. Moreover, failure to inquire specifically about the nature of post-high school training seems to lead to errors in placing people in the high school versus some college categories—whether the information comes from a respondent or a close relative. See Haberman and Sheinberg (1966).

12. Accurate here means within the same broad category, though virtually all correct responses specified the exact same major. For this comparison husbands and wives were combined since there are not enough in each category to justify controlling by sex.

Major	*Percent Correct*	N
Health	100	11
Engineering	91	23
Education	88	24
Natural sciences (incl. mathematics)	81	21
Business	76	29
Humanities and the arts	62	24
Social sciences	58	19

gineering, and education majors are very accurately perceived and reported by spouses. At the opposite extreme, those who major in the social sciences or humanities and the arts are often misclassified. Moreover, if we limit the comparison to those who completed college, majors in the social sciences, humanities and the arts, and business are still just as poorly reported.

There would seem to be relatively little that can be done to make these reports more accurate. It is unlikely that a probe would improve the responses, especially since the errors do not seem to follow any explicable pattern (such as confusing education majors who take a lot of history with history majors). Our results do, however, suggest caution in collecting and using information about spouses' college majors. If the sample is likely to contain numerous social science, humanities, or arts majors, spouses' reports would seem to be almost unusable.

Turning to occupations, we again find that spouses' reports are very accurate in nearly every category (table 6.2). The one excep-

Table 6.2
Accuracy of Wives' Reports of Spouse's Occupation

Husband's Occupation (own report)	Wife's Report of Husband's Occupation	
	Percent accurate	*Number of cases*
Professional and technical	93	69
Self-employed businessmen, managers and officials	87	111
Clerical and sales	83	48
Skilled	90	110
Semi-skilled operatives and kindred workers	92	68
Service workers	69	28
Unskilled (nonfarm) laborers	91	111
Farmers and farm laborers	97	22
Total	88	567

tion is service workers. It turns out, however, that over half of the errors in this category can be traced to a single coding error that classified a number of public administrators as service workers. Eliminating these cases makes 85 percent of the spouses' reports correct. Hence we can conclude that all categories of occupation are accurately reported by wives.

There is one aspect of employment that is poorly reported by spouses and, to a lesser extent, by respondents themselves. This is the matter of governmental employment. These data are shown in table 6.3 for both husbands' and wives' responses about each other.

Table 6.3
Accuracy of Husbands' and Wives' Reports on
Spouses' Employment by Government
(In percentages)

Worked for Government (own report)	Husband Worked for Government (as reported by wife)			Wife Worked for Government (as reported by husband)		
	Yes	*No*	*Total*	*Yes*	*No*	*Total*
Yes	59	41	29	53	47	18
No	4	96	71	2	98	82
Total	20	80	100	11	89	100
			N = 523			N = 516

The results are percentaged by rows, which emphasizes the inaccuracy in the "yes" category. If we were to percentage by the corner, we would find that from 85 percent in the case of the husband's employment, to 90 percent in the case of the wife's employment, agreed that the spouse did or did not work for the government. These high "total" percentages, however, are misleading if we are interested primarily in those who have worked for the government. Using the husbands' reports about the wives, we would be dealing with only a little over half of the females actually employed by the government. Results are not much better using the wives' reports about the husbands. Moreover, as the marginals show, this is the one case in which aggregate reports given by the spouses are substantially in error.

The source of these errors is very difficult to pin down. We initially assumed that much of the error might be traceable to current occupations (such as schoolteachers) about which there might be some ambiguity. There were only a few such cases, however. Next we looked at the time period of reported governmental employment. For those few cases in which the only employment was twenty-five or more years earlier, the spouses' reports failed to mention any governmental work. But aside from these extreme cases, the time of employment made little difference in accuracy of reporting. The length of employment did make some difference. Spouses' reports were accurate only about half as often when the respondent reported working for the government a year or less. These short-term jobs account for about a quarter of all the errors in spouses' reports.

Because we could not locate the errors more precisely, my suggestions for improvement must be quite general. The most useful step would probably be to split up the question both by respondent and time period. Thus one question would inquire about the respondent presently, one about the respondent in the past, one about the spouse presently, and one about the spouse in the past. Altogether, these suggestions would lead to some improvement in spouses' reports. I suggest, however, that more pretesting is needed to design good questions about spouses' governmental work and about respondents' and spouses' past employment generally.

Correlates of Accurate Spouses' Reports

With the high levels of accuracy observed, both overall and within particular categories, it is unlikely that many characteristics would correlate highly with the error found. Indeed this turned out to be correct for several features we might wish to explore. Whether the wife was employed or not made very little difference in the correlations observed, and the differences were in no way consistent. The race of the respondents had little effect, as did their education. The fact that the errors do not cluster around one type of respondent is further evidence that spouses' reports of demographic and related information can be relied upon in most instances.

There is, however, one characteristic that is likely to make a significant difference in the accuracy of husbands' and wives' reports. When individuals remarry, we might expect them to have correct information about their spouses somewhat less often. In addition, complications will sometimes arise, as they did with students and parents, over the precise referents of the questions. Our sample does not have the best design for studying the effects of remarriage. In fact, no question about remarriage was asked. However, respondents who reported that they were married seventeen years or less had very likely remarried. Seven percent of the respondents fell into this category. Another factor working against our analysis is that some of these apparent remarriages were of quite long standing. There is an almost rectangular distribution of two or three cases reporting one, two, and so on up to seventeen years of marriage. Hence we will not be able to look at those who were very recently remarried versus those who were remarried for longer periods of time.

These facts about our sample, along with the results in figure 6.2, suggest that some care must be exercised in gathering reports even of demographic information when significant number of remarriages are likely to be found in one's population. All of the correlations except for education and occupation are lower than the corresponding ones in figure 6.1. The drop in two correlations is particularly significant. Length of residence in the local community could differ for any husband and wife, but it seems especially likely in remarriages. Thus the especially low correlation for this characteristic is probably a reflection of true differences rather than misperceptions. A similar explanation seems likely for reports of subjective social class. A person who has been married for a long period of time and then remarries someone with a different occupation might not easily change subjective feelings such as class membership. Interestingly, then, we might get some situations where husband and wife understandably give different reports of their subjective class.

I do not wish to overemphasize the inaccuracies and disagreements among those who have remarried. Most of the correlations are still high enough to indicate widespread agreement. And reports of education and occupation, the most widely used characteristics, are just as accurately reported in this group. Moreover, since only a small proportion of the total sample is remarried, the correlations for the overall sample are hardly affected. Nevertheless, the fact that most of the observed correlations were lower for this group— where many of the remarriages were of five or ten or more years in duration—indicates that considerable caution is necessary in utiliz-

.94	Husband's education
.89	Wife's education
.88	Own home or renting
.87	Number of children in the family Number of years of husband's military service Husband works for himself, himself and someone else, or someone else
.84	Husband's occupation (SRC code)
.83	Length of marriage
.77	Husband's occupation (Duncan decile code)
.74	Anticipated family income
.70	Some family member belongs to a labor union
.53	Husband has worked for government at some time
.46	Wife has worked for government at some time
.30	Length of residence in local community
.27	Subjective social class

Figure 6.2
Tau-*b* Correlations between Husbands' and Wives'
Reports of Demographic and Related Information,
for Remarried Respondents
(N = 38)

ing spouses' reports when a significant number of remarriages, especially recent remarriages, is found. Questions that require some historical knowledge or perspective seem particularly susceptible to error and misperception.

Spouses' reports about demographic and related information, like students' reports about parents, can be used with confidence. This conclusion is based not only on the high overall correlations but also on the lack of bias in socially acceptable directions and on the accuracy of responses within particular categories. In addition, the consistently high correlations for subsets of the population (with those who have remarried as a possible exception) suggest that the same high rates of accuracy will characterize most types of samples.

The most important point to add to this conclusion is that specification of the husband and wife separately will often add a crucial amount of clarity both in the construction of questions and of codes. Our treatment of union membership illustrates the kind of problem to avoid in code construction. The question on length of residence in the local community indicates the need to consider the use of separate questions about the husband and wife. Upon reflection the point is fairly obvious. Nonetheless, all too often this fact is forgotten when questions about "the family" are designed. Particularly in dealing with certain types of populations, such as young couples, it must be remembered that the husband and wife may differ on a variety of family characteristics. The general point is that for both substantive and methodological purposes we must not assume that the family is homogeneous. Even on characteristics for which there is perforce some sharing, spouses may differ. Survey questions ignore this potential difference at the cost of some accuracy—more or less depending on the population in question.

Finally, my conclusion about agreement between spouses' reports does not extend to subjective social class. This measure showed the lowest overall agreement rates and was subject to the greatest fluctuations across control categories. It can hardly be considered a "family" characteristic since so many husbands and wives differed in their responses. Yet the notion of social class is usually attached to the family and not to each of its members individually. Thus it seems likely that for many families this measure fails to tap a highly stable, identifiable characteristic of the family.

Together with the results of the student-parent analysis, the present findings indicate that demographic and related factual information can in many cases be gathered from respondents closely related to the individual in question. If anything, however, we must take more care than usual to avoid potential errors and biases in formulating questions and codes. Some specific suggestions have been given along the way. The most general point, however, is that absolute clarity in specifying exactly which individual is in question and precisely what information is sought is essential, as well as a clear understanding on the part of the researcher about whether he is asking for an individual characteristic or one that is more truly invariant from one family respondent to another.

7: Reports of Spouses' Partisanship and Attitudes toward Political and Social Groups

In this chapter I treat spouses' reports of two distinct kinds of political measures. The first of these is partisanship, with which I dealt earlier for the student-parent case. The second measure is the so-called "thermometer" rating of individuals' feelings about important political and social groups. These ratings represent an important addition to the analysis of spouses' reports because it is a relatively new measurement technique and because it comes closer than any of our other variables to assessing specific political attitudes. Partisanship, of course, measures a kind of general orientation toward the political world, but it is well known that party identification differs in important ways from assessments of more particular attitudes. For example, people often admit to having no opinion on specific issues whereas few individuals fail to respond to the partisanship item. In addition, partisanship has been found to be more stable than other attitudes over an extended period of time (Converse, 1964). Thus it is important to be able to judge the reliability and validity of spouses' reports of measures other than party ties. Group evaluations will help fill this need.

Two other measures—the frequency of husband-wife political conversations and the frequency of disagreement over political issues—could conceivably be included in this chapter. I decided, however, that since they ask the respondent to assess family interaction and family agreement rather than characteristics of his or her spouse, they fit most appropriately into the following chapter on family structure and interaction, and I will treat them there.

NATURE OF THE DATA

In this chapter we will assume that respondents' reports about their partisanship as well as their evaluations of groups correctly reflect their own feelings, and we will speak of the accuracy of spouses' reports. This is a bit gratuitous in the case of group evaluations, since there is no evidence, such as panel data, to support the reliability of these ratings. And indeed our results will warn us of a possible unreliability. Nevertheless, since there is typically no external source for validating respondents' reports about themselves, we will assume that they are more or less free of error.

Questions Used in This Study

Party identification was tapped with the standard SRC question as indicated in chapter 3. Minimal modifications were needed in order to ask about the respondent's spouse.

The thermometer items were introduced with a lengthy preface. In addition, interviewers were instructed to take some time if necessary to be sure that respondents understood how the thermometer works. The preface read as follows:

> *There are many groups in America and we would like to get your feelings toward some of these groups. Here's a card* (Interviewer hands over card) *on which there is something we call a "feeling thermometer."*
>
> *Here's how it works. If you don't know too much about a group or don't feel particularly warm or cold toward them, then you should place them in the middle, at the 50° mark.*
>
> *If you have a warm feeling toward a group or feel favorably toward it, you would place it somewhere between 50° and 100°, depending on how warm your feeling is toward the group.*
>
> *On the other hand, if there are some you don't care for too much, then you would place them somewhere between 0° and 50°.*
>
> *Our first group is the labor unions. Where would you put them on the thermometer?*

In our study respondents were then asked about eight groups— labor unions, Southerners, Catholics, big business, Jews, whites, Protestants, and Negroes.

Spouses' ratings were obtained immediately afterward with the following question:

Now I'm going to read the list again. This time I would like you to place the groups on the thermometer according to how you think your wife (husband) feels toward them. If you don't have any idea how she (he) might feel, just say so. The first group is labor unions. Where do you think your wife (husband) would place them on the thermometer?

In this case separate codes were used to indicate "don't know how he or she feels" and "doesn't know too much about a group" (50°).

Two-digit ratings were coded, using 99° for a rating of 100°. In practice, most ratings are 50° and over, and virtually no one used ratings other than every five or ten degrees (such as 50°, 55°, 60°, etc.).

AGGREGATE COMPARISONS

Almost all respondents are able to report the perceived partisanship of their spouses. Only 4 percent of the husbands and 2.5 percent of the wives failed to report the spouses' party loyalties. Aggregate comparisons of the reports are displayed in figure 7.1. They indicate what we have by now come to expect, namely that the proportion of Independents is underestimated.[1] What is surprising, however, is the magnitude of the underestimates. Spouses' reports are thought to be highly accurate, and aggregate comparisons often obscure what inaccuracies there are. Thus it was not expected that discrepancies of this size would appear in husbands' and wives' reports.

Indeed the discrepancies in wives' and especially in husbands' reports are larger than the errors previously observed in student perceptions. This occurs even though we shall see below that at an individual level spouses' reports are more accurate than students'. This apparent anomaly can be explained by a careful analysis of the figures given below on accuracy of reports within categories of partisanship. Understandable or not, however, it underscores the

1. The ratio of Democrats to Republicans is quite well preserved in spouses' reports, but the relative proportions of strong to weak identifiers are not well matched.

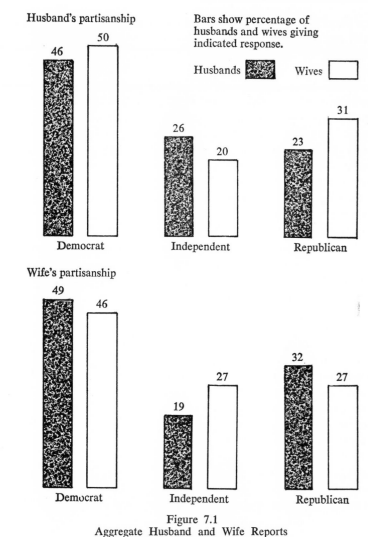

Figure 7.1
Aggregate Husband and Wife Reports
of Spouse's Party Identification

fact that reports about others' partisan identities, even by spouses, are likely to seriously underreport the incidence of Independence.[2] And any increase in the true proportion of Independents, as occurred in the late sixties, is likely to exacerbate this problem (see below).

In the aggregate, reports of spouses' group evaluations suffer more from lack of response than from errors in responses given. On the average 7 percent of the husbands and 10 percent of the wives simply said that they did not know how their spouses would rank each group. For both spouses big business was the group most often unrated, 11 percent of the husbands and 15 percent of the wives not giving a spouse's rating. For most groups the percentage of "don't knows" is higher than for virtually any of the other demographic, political, or family characteristics analyzed elsewhere in this book.

Despite the relatively high rate of DK responses, the reports that are given are very accurate in the aggregate. This conclusion applies to virtually all of the groups, to reports from both spouses, and to a variety of comparisons that we might wish to make. The data are provided in table 7.1. For each group the table shows the mean rating given by husbands and wives about themselves and about their spouses. Since a rating of 50° is used to indicate lack of any real feeling about a group as well as a middle-range feeling, and it might be used especially to guess about spouses' ratings, I have also provided the percentage of respondents using this rating. Of the sixteen comparisons that can be made of the mean ratings, the difference is larger than three degrees in only one case. This is true of blacks, where husbands rate them 66.6° and wives estimated husbands' ratings at five degrees lower. Similarly, the percentage of 50° ratings is accurately reported in each case except big business, where wives overestimate and husbands underestimate the use of that rating by their spouses. Standard deviations of the mean rank-

2. The magnitude of the error in spouses' reports is perhaps best illustrated by referring to the widely noticed increase in the proportion of Independents in the late 1960s. The increase amounted to about 8% on the average—in other words, by about the same amount that Independence among wives' was underreported.

Table 7.1
Aggregate Husband and Wife Ratings of Political and Social Groups

| | Husbands' Ratings | | | | | |
| | Own report | | | As reported by wives | | |
	Mean score	*Standard deviation*	*% 50°*	*Mean score*	*Standard deviation*	*% 50°*
Labor unions	60.3	26.5	17	59.1	27.5	16
Southerners	66.3	23.3	24	64.3	24.8	23
Catholics	69.0	23.9	26	68.8	24.4	25
Big business	66.0	21.9	19	62.9	22.5	27
Jews	63.4	21.7	35	62.4	22.9	35
Whites	82.8	17.4	13	85.5	15.8	9
Protestants	82.0	17.4	14	82.6	18.2	12
Negroes	66.6	21.9	24	61.5	26.0	19

| | Wives' Ratings | | | | | |
| | Own report | | | As reported by husbands | | |
	Mean score	*Standard deviation*	*% 50°*	*Mean score*	*Standard deviation*	*% 50°*
Labor unions	56.1	23.9	28	57.9	24.3	29
Southerners	65.6	23.8	27	68.1	23.7	24
Catholics	71.0	23.6	26	68.1	24.6	24
Big business	60.9	19.7	37	64.3	20.2	30
Jews	65.3	21.2	35	64.4	20.7	34
Whites	85.1	16.6	10	83.4	17.6	12
Protestants	84.9	16.8	10	83.5	17.2	11
Negroes	66.8	21.8	24	65.3	23.5	25

ings are also very similar whether using the respondents' own reports or spouses' reports.

As a final comparison, we might wish to compare husbands and wives as reported separately or as reported by one or the other spouse alone. This comparison likewise suggests accurate reporting of spouses' ratings. It will be interesting to see whether this conclusion carries over to the individual comparisons below.

INDIVIDUAL COMPARISONS—PARTY IDENTIFICATION

The overall accuracy rates of husbands' and wives' reports of each other's partisanship are very high—.74 for wives' reports about their husbands and .71 for husbands' reports about wives. Except for reports of demographic characteristics and the direction of the parents' presidential vote, these are the highest accuracy rates observed and attest to the fact that on the whole spouses' party loyalties are accurately perceived and reported.

This is not to say that the reports contain no systematic errors. As with students' reports about parents and vice versa, there are

Table 7.2
Husbands' and Wives' Reports of Spouse's Party Identification
(In percentages)

Wife's Report	Husband's Partisanship (own report)						
	Strong Dem.	Weak Dem.	Ind. Dem.	Ind.	Ind. Rep.	Weak Rep.	Strong Rep.
Democrat	95	84	49	24	4	6	0
Independent	2	10	46	67	56	12	4
Republican	2	5	5	9	40	82	96
Total	99	99	100	100	100	100	100
N	116	117	47	43	38	85	57

Husband's Report	Wife's Partisanship (own report)						
	Strong Dem.	Weak Dem.	Ind. Dem.	Ind.	Ind. Rep.	Weak Rep.	Strong Rep.
Democrat	95	82	36	14	16	6	8
Independent	4	11	54	54	32	12	2
Republican	1	7	10	33	51	82	90
Total	100	100	100	101	99	100	100
N	90	137	53	46	30	68	64

considerable variations across the partisanship spectrum as shown in table 7.2.[3] For the most part these figures show the same pattern as students' reports about parents. For both spouses, accuracy rates dip as one moves away from strong partisans and then take a slight

3. The proportion of husbands and wives who did not know their spouses' party identification also varied by partisanship, as follows:

	Husband's Partisanship						
	Strong Dem.	Weak Dem.	Ind. Dem.	Ind.	Ind. Rep.	Weak Rep.	Strong Rep.
% of wives DK	0	1	2	10	5	0	3

	Wife's Partisanship						
% of husbands DK	1	5	7	4	0	5	1

upturn among pure Independents. Independent leaners are often classified as partisans of the party toward which they lean, but they are not very often put in the opposing party.[4] It is encouraging, of course, that in a year in which the short-term forces were so strongly Democratic, perceptions of partisanship do not seem to be biased in that direction.

What is perhaps most surprising about the variations in accuracy rates is that the percentages in the middle of the spectrum dip as low as they do. It is true that accuracy rates for spouses' reports are higher than those for students' reports in five out of the six comparisons that can be made using the Independent categories. However, in two additional categories—pure Independents among wives and Independent Democrats among husbands—the increase is not too large, especially considering the vast room for improvement over student accuracy rates. And it is still true that among Independents as a whole only a little over half of the respondents are correctly categorized by spouses. It is these relatively low levels of accuracy that account for the discrepancies in aggregate reports observed earlier. Few partisans are reported as Independents, but a larger proportion of Independents are thought of as partisans. This imbalance creates the low proportion of Independents as reported by spouses. Hence, for all the accuracy of spouses' reports, we must be alert to the effects of this systematic error. In addition, other things being equal, the seriousness of the error will be greater the larger the proportion of Independents in the population.

As we turn our attention to correlates of accurate reporting, we find a difference between husbands' and wives' reports. Husbands' reports reveal greater and more consistent variations than wives'

---

4. With accuracy interpreted as those reports within one category on either side of the spouse's report, the following figures are obtained:

	Husband's Partisanship						
	Strong Dem.	*Weak Dem.*	*Ind. Dem.*	*Ind.*	*Ind. Rep.*	*Weak Rep.*	*Strong Rep.*
% of wives accurate	95	91	78	67	74	86	96
	Wife's Partisanship						
% of husbands accurate	95	89	78	54	64	87	90

Table 7.3
Tau-*b* Correlations between Husbands' and Wives' Reports
of Spouse's Party Identification

Control Category	Wife's Report about Husband		Husband's Report about Wife	
	τ_b	N	τ_b	N
Education				
College	.81	108	.76	156
9–12 grades	.71	314	.72	220
0–8 grades	.69	77	.61	111
Frequency of conversations[a]				
High 1	.76	49	.85	45
2	.76	70	.84	72
3	.75	114	.68	111
4	.80	93	.73	86
5	.71	77	.60	79
Low 6	.68	88	.55	81
Political interest of respondent				
High	.75	209	.74	306
Medium	.76	173	.68	123
Low	.70	121	.61	58

[a] This is an index combining the husband's and wife's reports of the frequency of husband-wife political conversations.

reports. As can be seen in table 7.3 for three relevant controls, the correlations representing the wives' accuracy rarely fall below about .7. At the same time, the husbands' levels of accuracy fall off rather consistently when they have relatively little education, when they are relatively uninterested in politics, and when political conversations in the family are judged to be rather infrequent. Nor is the deterioration in husbands' accuracy due to a shift in wives' partisanship, particularly an increase in the number of Independents. I do not wish to overexaggerate the decline in the accuracy of husbands' reports. It is especially low only in the bottom categories of the three measures reported, which can be seen by the numbers of cases to represent less than a proportionate share of respondents. And even then the accuracy levels are on a par with overall student reports of parents. One good test of the meaningfulness of this reduced accuracy will be to see below whether self-directed bias is greater among these same groups.

Only one group shows markedly lower levels of accuracy for

both husbands' and wives' reports. Among blacks the correlations dip to .45 for the husbands' reports and .44 for the wives' reports. As with reports of students and parents, the low correlations can be traced directly to respondents who view their spouses as Democrats even when they report themselves to be Independents or Republicans. Once again it is significant that spouses' reports no less than students' and parents' reports about each other are touched by this factor. Notwithstanding the high overall accuracy rates at the individual level, we must not blind ourselves to the kind of error that can occur when the distribution of respondents is highly one-sided.

Another factor that could lead to sharply reduced accuracy levels is remarriage. Wives' reports are still very good for our sample of remarriages, the correlation being .77. In contrast, the correlation for husbands' reports drops to .59. Remembering that some of these remarriages represent terms of ten or fifteen years, caution is appropriate in samples where for some reason recent remarriages are quite frequent, for spouses' reports of political characteristics could prove rather unreliable.

Self-directed Bias in Husbands' and Wives' Reports

Curiously, while wives' reports are slightly more accurate than husbands' reports and show less variation across population groups, their reports are more biased in the direction of their own partisanship. Sixty-one percent of the erroneous reports given by wives are in the direction of the wife's own attitude. This is precisely the same percentage as observed in the students' reports. In contrast, 55 percent of the husbands' erroneous reports are in the direction of their own partisanship. The degree to which these biases overestimate the true husband-wife correlation can be seen in figure 7.2. If we use husbands' reports, the true correlation is overestimated by a mere .02, whereas the wives' reports overestimate the true figure by .07.

As with the students' reports, overestimates in various groups

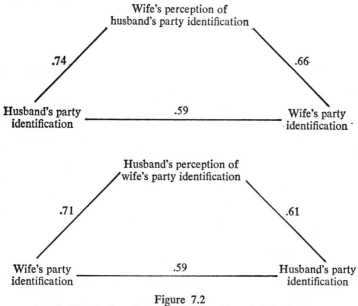

Figure 7.2
Tau-*b* Correlations between Husbands' and Wives' Party
Identification Using Spouses' Perceptions and Their Own Reports

within the population center around these overall figures.[5] Thus on
the average, wives' reports overestimate the true relationship by
four or five more points than do husbands' reports. Moreover, in
most control categories wives' reports yield the higher estimate.
Importantly, relationships such as that between education and simi-

5. The distribution of the overestimates of the husband-wife correlations
were as follows:

Amount of overestimate	≦−.04	−.03−−.01	0	.01–.03	.04–.06	≧.07
Number of control categories (husbands)	2 (12%)	2 (12%)	4 (25%)	4 (25%)	3 (19%)	1 (6%)
Number of control categories (wives)	0	0	0	3 (19%)	8 (50%)	5 (31%)

larity of husbands' and wives' partisanship are judged to be very much the same whichever reports were used.[6]

Self-directed bias does not seem to be concentrated in parts of the population where spouses' reports, especially from the husbands, were less accurate. Thus, for example, in the least-educated segment of the population the overestimates were very close to the average for the entire population. Again, of course, there are exceptions, such as among blacks where the overestimate is .19 for husbands' and .08 for wives' reports. Overall, we can most often expect spouses' reports to overestimate the true husband-wife similarity by between 0 and .06, with husbands' reports perhaps being a little more accurate.

INDIVIDUAL COMPARISONS—GROUP EVALUATIONS

The thermometer measure is intended to gather more interval-like measurements of individual feelings. Therefore in this section I will use Pearson correlations rather than tau-*b* correlations as a measure of the accuracy of spouses' reports. Lest there be any problem of interpretation, however, I have also divided the responses into decile scores and computed tau-*b* correlations. As expected, the Pearson correlations are somewhat higher, averaging .07 above the tau-*b* values. The rank order of the correlations as well as the comparisons between husbands' and wives' accuracy levels are very similar whichever correlational measure is used.

The correlations for both spouses' reports are given in figure 7.3. The most interesting point about the correlations is how closely the order of magnitude corresponds to the size of the standard deviations of respondents' own ratings as given in table 7.1. As the standard deviations and, hence, the variance of the ratings go up, so do the correlations. As the ratings are confined to a more narrow range, such as for whites and Protestants, the correlations decline

6. While the difference is found rather consistently in this sample, without further evidence I do not put much weight on the difference in the over-estimates from using wives' versus husbands' reports. Neither the data on groups, to be presented below, nor material on demographic characteristics or family characteristics suggest that wives' reports are particularly biased compared to husbands'.

Accuracy of wife's ratings		Accuracy of husband's ratings	
.58	Labor unions	.57	Catholics
.56	Catholics	.56	Labor unions
		.54	Southerners
.50	Southerners		
		.46	Jews
.45	Jews		Negroes
.44	Big business		
		.41	Big business
.40	Negroes		
		.34	Protestants
.33	Protestants	.33	Whites
.27	Whites		

Figure 7.3
Pearson Correlations between Husbands' and Wives'
Reports of Spouse's Group Evaluations

notably. Hence the ranking of the groups in figure 7.3 seems in large measure to be due to the variance of the rankings used to judge each group. It would be misleading under such circumstances to conclude that husbands and wives know each others' attitudes about labor unions, for example, better than each others' feelings about blacks or whites.

Several conclusions can, however, be drawn. For one thing, when the variance is fairly large, as for labor unions, the accuracy level of spouses' reports is reasonably high. Thus husbands and wives seem to know enough about spouses' feelings that they might be judged accurate enough reporters when there is considerable diversity of opinion about the matter in question (i.e., even greater than for labor unions). It is not always easy, of course, to know in advance just what will be controversial and hence show large variations in feelings. If we had had to guess, I suspect that we would have expected greater variance on the rating of blacks than on the rating of labor unions. And yet the opposite was true. Moreover for such groups as whites and Protestants, it is unlikely that we can even contrive a situation (see below) in which the variance of ratings would be high enough to achieve sufficient levels of accuracy in spouses' reports.

At the same time, the results suggest that increasing the variance in respondents' attitudes may be the key to achieving higher levels of accuracy in spouses' reports. If we can differentiate individuals into more and finer categories, at least one useful consequence would be a greater possibility of reliably using reports of spouses. As suggested above, this may not always be possible. As in the case of whites, it would probably be very difficult if not impossible to spread out respondents adequately. However, just as the thermometer measure itself serves to discriminate more finely than a question with two or three or four response categories, perhaps there are variations of thermometer-like items or of introductions to them that would serve the purpose of increasing the variance in individual judgments.

As it stands, with the variance actually obtained for each of these groups, the spouses' reports must be judged to be only moderately accurate at best, and rather poor in a number of cases. Even using the generally higher Pearson correlations, we find the very highest accuracy rating to be just below that of students' perceptions of their parents' partisanship. Moreover, we will see an additional problem below when we look at self-directed bias. Husbands and wives seem equally able to report spouses' group evaluations. Husbands' perceptions are on balance slightly more accurate, but the difference is not large enough to be meaningful.

The accuracy of both husbands' and wives' reports is clearly highest when the spouse reported a rating in the 50s or 90s. In these cases, about half or more of the spouses also placed the respondents in the 50s or 90s, respectively. In the other categories, accuracy rates were a third or less. Particularly striking is the inaccuracy when respondents rated a group very low. Of all the ratings below 50°, including extremely negative feelings, only 18 percent of the spouses placed the respondent in the same decile location. In addition, the errors that were made were often substantial. The tendency not to use ratings below the midpoint of the scale meant that spouses' reports were particularly poor when a respondent did choose such a rating. Again a slightly changed response format, in which respondents were less reluctant to use the lower end of the scale, might significantly improve the reliability of spouses' ratings.[7]

Given the differences in the correlations representing husbands' and wives' accuracy according to the variance in the respondents' own reports, it is unlikely that we will find many significant correlates of accurate ratings. For example, we might hypothesize that group members would more accurately perceive their spouses' rankings of that particular group. This would also seem to follow from the fact that group members have a tendency not to rank themselves very low, where the lowest accuracy rates are recorded. Nonetheless, accuracy levels among group members about spouses' ratings of their own group tend to be slightly lower than for spouses as a whole. This makes sense when we realize that the variance in respondents' ratings is likely to be reduced by using only group members. Despite the plausibility of the original hypothesis, then, accuracy of spouses' perceptions is not increased by group membership.

A similar argument holds if we control on other relevant characteristics. While there is no necessary reduction in the variance of ratings by a particular group, it is likely that a group which is homogeneous on, say, education would yield more homogeneous ratings than a group with more varying education levels. Consequently it is not too surprising that we do not find any groups in which the correlations representing husbands' and wives' accuracy levels are consistently higher than for the population as a whole. Here and there the correlations do rise, as we might expect given

7. The 7-point scales used recently by the Center for Political Studies of the University of Michigan might be a useful step in this direction. While it might seem a long way from the thermometer to 7-point scales, the tendency to use ratings of 5° and especially 10° means that the thermometer scale in effect is more like an 11-point scale (0, 1, . . . , 10) in which only the 6 ratings from 5 through 10 are frequently used. A glance at the codebook for the 1970 National Election Study shows that all 7 ratings of the 7-point scales are used quite freely.

different proportions of 50° and 90° ratings, varying proportions of ratings below 50°, and differing amounts of variance. And we cannot rule out the possibility that accuracy levels would be very high under some particular configurations of circumstances. However, given the particular groups rated here, the way they were viewed in the mid-sixties, and so on, it appears unlikely that accuracy rates will be high enough to be really useful in any major social groupings.

Self-directed Bias in Husbands' and Wives' Reports

The most astounding feature of husbands' and wives' reports of each others' group ratings is the degree to which perceptions of the spouse are biased in the direction of one's own feelings. Table 7.4

Table 7.4
Pearson Correlations between Husbands' and Wives' Group
Evaluations Using Spouses' Perceptions and Their Own Reports

Group	Similarity Using Wives' Reports	Similarity Using Husbands' Reports	Similarity (actual)
Labor unions	.78	.72	.48
Southerners	.82	.80	.45
Catholics	.80	.81	.46
Big business	.70	.72	.30
Jews	.84	.84	.37
Whites	.92	.90	.24
Protestants	.81	.84	.27
Negroes	.74	.75	.35

shows the correlations between husbands' and wives' own reports as well as the correlations between husbands and wives as seen by each spouse alone. The actual similarities are overestimated by a low of .24 and by a high of .68. This is far greater bias than we have seen in any other reports, even in cases such as parents' political interest, where overall accuracy levels were very low. For some reason it appears that when spouses' ratings were inaccurately perceived, homogeneity with oneself was most often assumed. Obviously this was true to nowhere near the same extent for party identification, so the question must be raised as to whether these very considerable overestimates are common to most political attitudes other than partisanship or whether they are peculiar to the thermometer item. We will return to this below.

The extent of the overestimates varies from one group to another, but it is always rather high. Even in the most favorable instances, where actual similarity was judged the highest, couples were seen as being still much more similar. Indeed, using perceived similarity we would argue that homogeneity was by far the norm, whereas in actuality heterogeneity seems to be a very frequent condition.[8] Moreover, overestimates were very high as seen by both husbands and wives. Neither spouses' reports seems to escape from the tremendous degree of self-directed bias.

The magnitude of the overestimates as well as their variability indicate that unlike partisanship, voting, and even political interest, it would be very risky to use spouses' reports in order to estimate similarity between husbands and wives. It seems likely that this conclusion also extends to other pairs of respondents such as students and parents.

With regard to party identification our results were mainly of a positive sort. At the individual level, accuracy rates were high enough to feel secure most often in using spouses' reports as if they were the actual reports from husbands or wives of respondents. Self-directed bias was usually low enough and consistent enough that gross errors of interpretation would not result from comparing respondents' own reports with their perceptions of their spouses.

I did caution, however, against assuming that no care need be taken in working with spouses' reports of partisanship. I indicated how aggregate levels of independence among spouses were relatively poorly estimated despite the high overall accuracy levels. I might emphasize here that this error is likely to be more or less serious depending on the type of sample involved and the particular timing of a study. Among young adults, for example, where Independents are frequent, reports from spouses would very likely underestimate that proportion by a good deal. With an otherwise comparable sample of older respondents, the underestimate would

8. The ranking of groups by actual similarity can be seen to be partly a function of the variances in the ratings just as were accuracy levels. This should be kept in mind.

be smaller and even perhaps nonexistent. Similarly, samples taken in the late sixties in contrast to earlier years would likewise show greater underestimates of the proportion of Independents when using spouses' reports. This is true because the proportion of Independents in the population had risen significantly.

Importantly, we can sometimes use the information presented in this chapter to make sensible corrections for biases that may exist in other samples. Thus, for example, if we assume that the internal cells in table 7.2, representing accuracy within categories of partisanship, remain the same, we can use these figures to make some reasonable estimates of the amount of bias likely to be found in reports that are actually received.[9] Even if the specific entries cannot be considered stable but the same pattern of accuracy is assumed, some inferences can still be made about the direction and probable amount of bias to be expected. Overall, then, while our results show high accuracy levels for spouses' reports of partisanship, they can also serve as a means to take corrective action for what inaccuracies are likely to exist.

My conclusions are not so sanguine when it comes to spouses' reports of thermometer ratings. Accuracy levels were not only much lower than for partisanship, but the degree of self-directed bias was so large as to seriously threaten any use of these reports. I suggested some corrective action to increase the variance in measures of respondents' attitudes. It is likely, however, that this would be only a partial corrective.

Because of the newness of the thermometer scales, I am necessarily less conclusive in the results here than in the case of most other measures I have used. On the one hand, it is possible that husbands and wives simply do not know with any degree of accuracy how their spouses feel about political issues. They may simply assume that their mates are very much like themselves. This is suggested by the relatively high rate of DK responses as well as by the tremendous self-directed bias observed.

A second possibility is that marriage partners by and large know their spouses' feelings about political attitudes but do not know

9. The same point obviously applies to tables 3.3 and 4.2 for youths' and parents' reports, respectively, of party identification and to tables 3.1 and 3.2 for youths' reports of parental voting.

their generalized feelings about whole groups. Alternatively, there may be few groups for which most respondents know how their spouses feel. In other words, for one group a subset of the population may know very adequately how their spouses feel while many others have no idea of their spouses' attitudes. On some other issue another, perhaps overlapping, portion of the population know their spouses' feelings, while the remainder do not. Hence no group reveals high levels of overall accuracy even though in each case there are subsamples with very accurate knowledge. (Admittedly the likelihood of this is lessened by the failure to find correlates of accurate reports.)

A final possibility is that the thermometer item itself is simply not a reliable or valid method for getting group evaluations. Respondents' reports about themselves, much less those about their spouses, may not reliably and accurately reflect their true feelings about the groups in question. There is no way without much further analysis, and perhaps even additional data such as from a panel study, to determine whether this is more than a mere possibility. At the very least, however, our results strongly urge that respondents not be used to report about others' group evaluations. More positively, they suggest strongly that efforts be made to determine the reliability of the measure for gathering data about respondents themselves.

Whichever is the case—whether respondents do not know their spouses' political attitudes generally, whether they are simply ignorant of spouses' feelings about groups, or whether the thermometer measure itself is unreliable—the results suggest fruitful areas for further inquiry as well as lead to some positive suggestions about the uses of respondents' reports and about data collection methods in general.

8: Family Structure and Relationships among Family Members

Comparison of student and parent reports of family characteristics showed remarkably little agreement about the nature of the family. This conclusion does not automatically generalize to a comparison of husbands' and wives' reports. There are good reasons to expect more agreement in the perceptions of husbands and wives. For example, to the etxent that student-parent disagreement is a reflection of generational differences, spouses should more often judge family traits in a similar way. In addition, parents have lived together as adults for a long period of time and have necessarily had to come to some agreement about methods of family decision making, about methods of child rearing, and so on. The comparison of accuracy rates for demographic and political data also suggests that more agreement might be expected between mothers and fathers than between students and parents—perhaps to the point that such data from parents could be considered reasonably valid descriptions of the family. Finally, some prior research has found considerable similarity between husbands' and wives' reports (Heer, 1962; Straus, 1969, p. 261) although more contradictory evidence has been found in small-scale studies (Kohn and Carroll, 1960; Wilkening and Morrison, 1963; Ballweg, 1969; Grandbois and Willett, 1970).

In this chapter we will also be able to compare levels of agreement on a few characteristics about which only parents were asked. Moreover, it will now make sense to examine as possible correlates of agreement certain background features that were irrelevant in the student-parent case. The primary example is education, where we can now see whether spouses with particular educational levels hold a common perception much more often than average.

Nature of the Data

As in the student-parent comparisons, I will speak here of levels of agreement between the spouses rather than of accuracy rates. Neither spouse's reports will be considered definitive. The one point that needs to be added to what was said in chapter 5 concerns the fine line drawn between what are considered family traits and what are considered characteristics of individual members or pairs of family members. For example, I will not include in this chapter the parents' perceptions of how well they and their students get along with one another, nor reports of disagreements between parents and students. I exclude these on the grounds that father-child and mother-child relationships may vary significantly within the same family and that the parents' questionnaire asked only about "you (the respondent) and your son or daughter." On the other hand, I include in this chapter a question that asks whether "you" want to have quite a lot to say about your sons' or daughters' friends, etc., on the grounds that intervention in the child's affairs is more a family matter than a matter for each parent alone.

This distinction seems to be in accord with common practices in other studies. In particular, studies of student-parent agreement often distinguish between the two parents, and closeness to each parent is often determined. But aspects of discipline and rule making within the family seem to be regarded as collective features (as, for example, in Maccoby et al., 1954; Almond and Verba, 1963; Middleton and Putney, 1963; Langton, 1969, p. 25). I feel, however, that this distinction is usually not so clear in practice, and I have indicated throughout the need for clarity in the referents of questions about the family. Nevertheless, past usage is sufficient to justify inclusion and exclusion for purposes of this chapter.

Questions Used in This Study

All but two of the items used in this chapter were given in chapter 5. The first new item is a sequence of questions concerning frequency of discussions and of disagreements about politics.

Do you and your wife (husband) ever talk about any kind of public affairs and politics, that is, anything having to do with local, state, national, or international affairs? (If yes) *Is this very often, pretty often, or not very often? Do you happen to recall a couple of things you have talked about lately?*

The 80 percent of the respondents who talked about politics at least sometimes were asked:

Do you and your wife (husband) ever disagree about anything having to do with public affairs and politics? (If yes) *Would you say that you disagree frequently, occasionally, or seldom? When you do disagree, what is it usually about?*

The other new item introduced here concerns family rule making:

Families differ in what kinds of rules, if any, they have for their teenagers. Are there any rules which have applied to your son (daughter) for the past two or three years? (If yes) *How did you go about deciding on these rules? Was it pretty much something you decided yourself, did you talk about them with your son (daughter), did you discuss them with other parents? Just how did you do it?*

The latter, open-ended question was coded in terms of which family member or members took part in making the decision.

AGGREGATE COMPARISONS

In the aggregate the family was described in quite similar terms by students and parents. This similarity of overall perceptions is even more true of husbands' and wives' reports. Aggregate responses to most of the items are given in figure 8.1. The differences average only 3.5 percent and are as large as 5 percent in only two cases. In most cases the differences are smaller than the already narrow differences observed for students and parents (fig. 5.1).

Neither the husband nor the wife seems to portray the family in a more favorable light. Sometimes one and sometimes the other spouse more frequently gives what might be regarded as a favorable response. The largest differences in perceptions occur

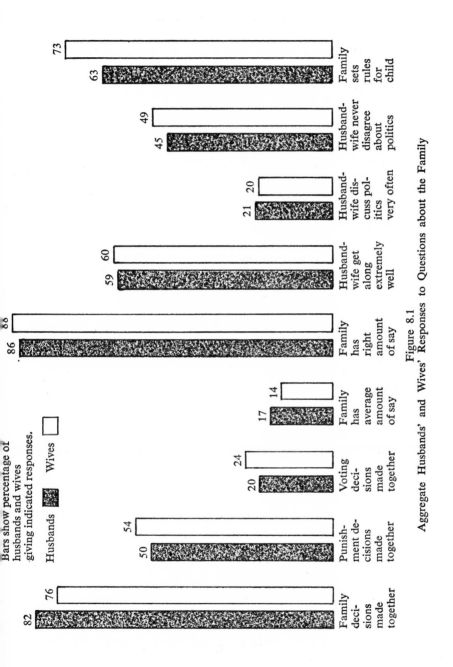

Bars show percentage of husbands and wives giving indicated responses.

Husbands ☐   Wives ▨

Family decisions made together	Punishment decisions made together	Voting decisions made together	Family has average amount of say	Family has right amount of say	Husband-wife get along extremely well	Husband-wife discuss politics very often	Husband-wife never disagree about politics	Family sets rules for child

Family decisions made together — 82, 76
Punishment decisions made together — 50, 54
Voting decisions made together — 20, 24
Family has average amount of say — 17, 14
Family has right amount of say — 86, 88
Husband-wife get along extremely well — 59, 60
Husband-wife discuss politics very often — 21, 20
Husband-wife never disagree about politics — 45, 49
Family sets rules for child — 63, 73

Figure 8.1
Aggregate Husbands' and Wives' Responses to Questions about the Family

over parent-child relationships, where the mother sees somewhat more frequent parental involvement. Even here, however, a solid majority of both parents say that the family does set rules for the child. And in a related comparison the difference is still smaller, in that 40 percent of the husbands and 46 percent of the wives say that the family has a lot to say in the child's affairs.

Several additional comparisons support the conclusion that husbands and wives provide similar aggregate pictures of the family. Neither spouse, for example, sees the family as being maternally or paternally dominated to a greater extent, either in general or in regard to more specific decisions about punishment of children and about voting. Similarly, when the husband and wife do disagree about politics, the frequency of disagreements is reported very similarly by each spouse.

Responses to open-ended questions about the subjects of political conversations and disagreements are also very similar for the most part. If responses are divided into the broad categories of world affairs, national affairs, state affairs, local affairs, civil rights, and other responses, very nearly the same proportions of husbands and wives report conversations dealing with each of these topics. Even in terms of more detailed categories, such as discussions about local schools, the proportions are the same. Using the same categories to characterize political disagreements, we see aggregate agreement between spouses about most of the topics. The only major difference is that husbands report disagreements about local affairs some 19 percent of the time compared to only 10 percent of the time for the wives. Conversely, 22 percent of the wives but only 10 percent of the husbands mention a disagreement about civil rights.

There is one topic on which substantial and understandable differences appear in the spouses' reports. The difference is no doubt due to the question format, and it is useful to observe for this reason. The question about how rules are made for the child was coded in terms of which family members were involved in the decision making. Both spouses reported that only one parent was involved about a quarter of the time. According to the husband, however, he made the decisions most of the time (19 percent of the cases in which rules were made at all) and the wife seldom made the decisions (3 percent). From the wife's point of view, the husband was involved very little (4 percent of the time), while she very often made the decisions (22 percent). These differences can be traced quite easily to the failure of the question to specify precisely which spouse or spouses were involved in deciding upon the rules.[1] I believe that if the question had referred specifically to the spouse as well as the respondent, husbands' and wives' reports would show substantial agreement. This is another indication, then, that questions about the family must indicate explicitly which family member or members are to be considered in answering the question. Assumptions that the referents are implicitly clear are likely to be false.

INDIVIDUAL COMPARISONS

The correlations between husbands' and wives' reports of family characteristics are given in figure 8.2. In every case in which a direct comparison can be made, except for television viewing, the correlations are higher than the comparable student-parent figures given in chapter 5. Still, the correlations are not too high—not high enough in my judgment to be satisfied by the measurement procedures. The very highest correlation is about on a par with reports of subjective social class, to which I raised serious objections in chapter 6.

Moreover, other considerations are not very encouraging. The ordering of items does not suggest that particular subsets of the questions are very good or very bad. For example, questions exclusively about husbands and wives versus those involving parents and children do not show uniformly more agreement. Similarly, a division along behavioral versus affective lines does not reveal areas of particularly high or low agreement. Another relevant point is the comparison of reports about the frequency of husband-wife discussions and disagreement about public affairs and politics. While still rather general questions, the subject matter is narrowed to one broad area. The fact that both of these correlations are relatively high might be mildly encouraging, but their magnitude

---

1. This is also indicated by the fact that it was impossible to tell which family members were involved in about 15% of the cases.

.50	How well husband-wife get along with each other
.44	Frequency of husband-wife discussions about politics
.40	Husband-wife disagreement on public affairs and politics Whether family sets rules for child
.34	How much say family has in child's affairs How decisions on voting are made
.31	How decisions on punishment of children are made
.27	How family decisions are made
.22	Whether husband and wife listen to radio with family
.18	Whether family has right amount of say in child's affairs
.05	Whether husband and wife watch television with family

Figure 8.2
Tau-*b* Correlations between Husbands' and Wives'
Reports of Family Structure and Interaction

suggests that limiting questions to one subject matter will not by itself lead to high rates of husband-wife agreement.

Spouses' reports of the subject matter of political conversations and disagreements further substantiate the lack of agreement. For this purpose we again used the broad categories of world affairs,

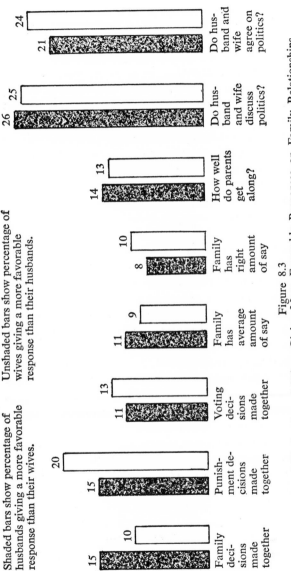

Shaded bars show percentage of husbands giving a more favorable response than their wives.

Unshaded bars show percentage of wives giving a more favorable response than their husbands.

15	15	13	11	14	26	21	
10	20	13	9	10	13	25	24

Family decisions made together · Punishment decisions made together · Voting decisions made together · Family has average amount of say · Family has right amount of say · How well do parents get along? · Do husband and wife discuss politics? · Do husband and wife agree on politics?

Figure 8.3

Percentage of Husbands and Wives Giving More Favorable Responses on Family Relationships national affairs, state affairs, local affairs, and civil rights matters. We also limited the comparison to husband-wife pairs in which both spouses mentioned discussions about politics or both mentioned that they disagreed about some political topic. Even so, when one spouse reported a particular subject, the other spouse reported the same topic only about half the time in any of the two or three responses that were coded. Calculating cell entries on the basis of the marginals indicates that the frequency of husband-wife agreement is no higher than would be expected by chance. In addition, no single category shows outstanding agreement by spouses. And even in the case of disagreements, in which the comparison is limited to less than 30 percent of the total sample (and far fewer in which one spouse mentions any particular category), husband-wife agreement is no higher than chance leads us to expect.

We can conclude that the lack of agreement observed earlier between students and parents is only marginally generational in origin, for when we observe parents—who share an "adult" perspective on family life and who perhaps share more family experiences than parents and children—we still find considerable disagreement as to the nature of family characteristics. We cannot, then, view the family simply as dual in nature, one type as perceived by the older generation and another type as perceived by the younger generation. Rather, data about family characteristics seem subject to a more fundamental problem.

Before considering the implications of our results, we should briefly examine two questions that were examined in more detail in the student-parent comparisons. First of all, is there observable bias such that husbands or wives consistently give more favorable responses about family features? The absence of generational considerations and the greater similarity of husbands' and wives' than of students' and parents' aggregate responses suggests that little bias ought to be found. Indeed this is the case, as shown clearly in figure 8.3. Husbands and wives each give more favorable responses exactly half of the time. And in no case are the differences very large or meaningful. In no way can we attribute the lack of agreement about family attributes to sex differences or family role differences between husbands and wives.

Finally, we can consider whether there are any correlates of husband-wife agreements, possibly suggesting subsets of families in which agreement is high or suggesting reasons for lack of overall agreement. One of the prime considerations was whether education would make a difference, either in the sense that high education would somehow contribute to greater sharing of perspectives or that similarity of education at whatever level would lead to common perceptions. In neither way did education make any consistent difference. Correlations between husbands' and wives' reports were occasionally higher among the highly educated, but they were just as often lower. When parents had a common education level, the correlations between their reports averaged, if anything, slightly less than the overall figures.

Results with other controls proved just as disappointing. It was expected, for example, that even in this sample black families might have been sufficiently more disrupted so that agreement between husband and wife would be consistently lower. Actually, however, the correlations turned out to be higher than those for the overall population more often than not, although the differences were usually not very large. Similarly, agreement was no higher in families in which there was only one child. In all cases the results were no more consistent if we limited the comparison to questions dealing solely with the husband and wife or to questions treating decision making about the children or parent-child interaction.

While it is always possible that there exist some correlates which were not considered, the results of our analysis of both husbands and wives and students and parents suggests that there is little hope of finding significant subsets of the population in which family members record high agreement in reporting observations about the family.

IMPLICATIONS OF THE FINDINGS

The comparisons we have made between husbands' and wives' and between students' and parents' responses to a diverse set of similarly worded questions adds to a growing body of evidence that documents an impressive lack of intrafamily agreement about family characteristics. The present analysis suggests further that the lack of agreement cannot be laid to generational differences, to sex or family role differences, or for the most part, to easily correctable faults in question design. Nor can we be more optimistic about the level of agreement to be expected in other, narrower types of samples.

The most encouraging results may be that differences in reporting family features do not seem to be generational in character or due to sex role differences. Hence in the aggregate, husbands' and wives' descriptions were remarkable similar and student and parent descriptions were mostly the same. For some descriptive purposes, then, the results are mildly encouraging. Studies relying totally on reports of husbands or wives or parents or youths are likely to arrive at very similar accounts of family living. It is necessary, of course, to exercise care. For example, in chapter 5 I indicated how descriptions of intergenerational change in family structure can be affected by the use of one rather than two or more respondents. Similarly, the consistent tendency of parents to somewhat overestimate family harmony and underreport less desirable qualities should be considered when evaluating data from parents alone. Nonetheless, the implications of our analyses are less serious for aggregate descriptive accounts of the family than for theoretical and analytical concerns.

The implications of our findings for theory and analysis are far-reaching. The lack of agreement among different members about the nature of the family unit demonstrates the failure of respondents' reports to give us accurate reports of family structure and interaction. Together with the absence of other adequate measurement techniques, it reveals our inability to measure family characteristics validly. Thus, our measurements of key analytic variables are very imperfect, and analyses relying on these measurements will be "suggestive" or "approximate" at best and very misleading at worst.

In chapter 5 I noted that some researchers would take exception to this line of reasoning. They would argue that whether or not respondents' reports accurately reflect the actual family situation is irrelevant, since the key variables are perceptions anyway. For example, it is not the real locus of power or the true relationship between father and son that is important; the crucial factor is how these characteristics are perceived. What really affects one's behavior, so the argument goes, is what one perceives, not the real situation.

The chief problem with this argument is that attempts to link the family theoretically with a host of dependent variables are often couched in behavioral rather than cognitive terms. For example, whether or not the student is allowed to participate in family decision making is often posited as crucial to performance and later participative roles because the experience gathered in the family is transferable to those other roles. Similarly when parents and children feel close to each other, parents supposedly have a greater influence on their offspring because of more frequent family interaction. Or again, the extent of husband and wife agreement is said to affect the development of a child's opinions because it is a partial measure of the homogeneity or heterogeneity of the family environment. Or finally, how well family members get along with each other is thought to be related to the child's development because it indicates the degree of conflict and tension in the home.

Each of these suggested linkages between the family and child or adult socialization carries a definite behavioral cast. Valid attempts to assess them can hardly be made using very imperfect measures of the family behavior implied. This does not mean that any or all of the above hypotheses are wrong—only that the usual data collected from the family are inadequate to test them. Nor does it imply that subjective observations about the family are useless. The argument that perceptions are as important as facts has some truth to it. Moreover, some of the above hypotheses can be stated in terms implying cognitive linkages. For example, students who feel that they are close to their parents may be more highly influenced by them because they are more willing to accept the parents' opinions uncritically.

We cannot, however, solve the problem simply by restating our hypotheses in cognitive terms. Whether it is acknowledged or not, if behavioral and cognitive elements work together to produce family effects, attempts to estimate the magnitude of relationships between family variables and dependent attitudes or behavior will be constantly frustrated by the reliance on perceptions alone. Unless adequate means can be devised to measure family variables, analyses of the role of the family in the political socialization process and perhaps even judgments about its relative importance will be unreliable.

The argument that only perceptions are relevant encounters another difficulty if we think about altering family behavior. If different members do not agree on what the family is like, there is no guarantee that changes are even attacking the right problem. Thus, the father who feels he is "too far" from his son and tries to remedy the situation may find that he makes things worse because the son feels they are too close already. Feedback, of course, *might* soon tell this father that something was amiss. But the whole thrust of our results is that such interchange about perceptions of family interaction is generally not sufficient to assure agreement among family members.

Our results are all the less satisfying because they do not give many clues as to how to make reports of family characteristics better, or even whether sufficient improvement is possible. Frankly, at this point I am not in a position to give unfailing advice on how to design adequate family measurements. What I can do, however, is simply to give a number of suggestions for possible improvements. I look on these as guidelines that might be tested with further methodological research.

The strongest and most specific suggestion I can make is that questions about the family and about family members should specify explicitly which individuals are to be considered in answering each question. Naturally this assumes a prior point—that of determining on theoretical grounds the basis on which a question should be answered. Does the researcher want the respondent to consider his or her spouse when answering questions such as whether "you" set rules for your child or how "you" and your child get along? When inquiring about what "the family" does together, does the researcher mean all family members or at least one parent and one child or what? If we are considering family decision making, are the husband and wife the sole participants or should the children be considered an integral part of the decision-making unit? Does it make any difference whether there is only a single child or whether the child involved is nearly an adult? It seems to me that these and similar questions are rarely considered explicitly. Yet our analysis suggested that clarification would have eliminated some of the ambiguity in the questions. Specifically because the family is not a single or perhaps even a homogeneous unit, precise specification seems necessary.

A second suggestion is that in designing and analyzing questions about the family we more often give consideration to dimensional techniques, such as scaling and factor analysis, that help determine whether responses to individual items are measuring the same concept. Methodological investigations of concepts such as political efficacy and trust, as well as substantive investigations of these concepts, have often used this approach. In contrast, measurements of family characteristics seem to use one of two other approaches. One approach is the single-shot technique, using a single question or a set of questions that are not combined in any way at the analysis stage. Alternatively, a series of questions is asked, such as decision making in a whole host of situations, but little attempt is made at the analysis stage to determine which of these measurements fits with which other ones and whether some of them should be excluded altogether from the measurement of a particular concept. As with political characteristics, it is likely that components that "obviously" go together as part of a larger concept will very often prove to fit together much less perfectly than expected.

An example of this procedure might be the determination of maternal domination in family decision making. Rather than dividing families into those which are maternally dominated and those which are paternally dominated, we might conceive of a continuum of maternal domination. Moreover, when the mother is not the determining factor, families may be divided more or less randomly between father dominance and equal decision-making power. Thus for some purposes an appropriate dichotomy may be between mother dominance and lack of mother dominance rather than between mother versus father dominance. In addition, maternal domination in some decision-making areas may not be highly correlated with maternal decision making in other areas. Whether these areas should be combined into a single measurement is a question that should be determined more consciously and on the basis of more analysis than typically seems to be the case.

Two other techniques that I can suggest would help spread out the distribution of families on our measurements, which is a worthy goal in itself, and might thereby help improve the validity of responses. There was a definite reluctance on the part of respondents to indicate that family members are not really very close or that they do not get along very well. With the questions used, this meant that a large proportion of the respondents wound up in a single "moderate" or "average" category. One procedure which has been used to make respondents feel that a socially disapproved response is more appropriate is to provide a prefatory remark that sanctions the less desirable response. Illustrations are provided in regard to political questions by the query on voting (see chapter 3) and on parents' reports about the child's party identification (chapter 4). Perhaps an analogous preface should be used for questions about the family, such as: "In the ideal family everyone supposedly gets along perfectly. In reality, we know that in some families people get along with each other very well while in other families they are not very compatible. How is it in your family; do you get along . . . ?" Such a preface, along with careful choosing of words such as "incompatible" rather than "not getting along very well" might remove some of the hesitancy about reporting poor family relations when they in fact exist.

The second step to spread out respondents might be to use a response format that allowed for more than three or four responses. Variations on the semantic differential have been tried with some success in other areas such as getting people's opinions on policy items, and a similar approach might be tried for questions about the family. Thus for example the respondent might be asked to place himself on a seven-point scale on which the end points were labeled "parents get along extremely well" and "parents are not very compatible." There would still presumably be a reluctance to choose the extreme end points, especially on the not very compatible end, but with seven or so points to choose from, the distribution might be more spread out than when there are only three or four categories to begin with.

These two steps to spread out respondents might improve validity of responses by at least a small amount. While percentage agreement between two or more respondents might actually decrease because of an increase in the number of categories, disagreements would perhaps be very small. Respondents previously had to choose between categories such as "extremely well" or "moderately well" even if they felt that the real situation was on the borderline of these two categories. With a larger set of responses, respondents would not be forced into one or the other of these categories and agreement—though not necessarily the proportion of perfect matches—might be improved. The end points of the scale would, I hope, be reserved for families that clearly deviated from the norm in either direction.

Finally, it is perhaps a truism that methods other than closed-ended survey questions should be tried. However, I am thinking particularly of methods that lend themselves to the survey situation or to minor adaptations thereof. For example, open-ended questions might provide considerably more insight into family decision making than even a long series of closed-ended items. Of course it is very difficult to rank a set of individuals on any measurement on the basis of open-ended questions, but this possibility should not be overlooked. Alternatively, one might use exploratory studies with open-ended questions as a means to developing improved closed-ended questions.

Another possible technique that can be used in connection with surveys is that of having respondents keep diaries for a specified period of time. Normally diaries are used simply to record what an individual does during the specific interval of time. It is possible, however, that a diary could be constructed that called for reports of interaction with other family members. Presumably the informant would not be called upon to make decisions such as "this indicates that we are compatible (or incompatible)," but records of such things as what disagreements actually occurred and what was done in the end might prove to be a useful means of analytically classifying families. If diaries are passed out and explained during an interview and then picked up later by the same interviewer, who can immediately check for clarity and completeness, problems associated with mailed-in material could in large measure be avoided.

In conclusion, the problem of gathering reliable and valid data about family characteristics is a profound one and calls for greater theoretical clarity, more frequent use of analytic techniques, and the development of new, imaginative data-gathering methods. It is not likely that any of the suggestions made above will by itself work the kind of improvement that is necessary. I hope, however, that they are a step in the right direction, since we have so far to go to achieve requisite levels of reliability and validity.

9: Summing Up and a Brief Look Ahead

The recent surge of interest in political socialization has resulted in a considerable expansion of empirical research relating the family to the political development of children. This expansion is evident in both the increasing number of studies devoted to the topic and the widening scope of inquiry. Many studies have utilized information about respondents' social and political backgrounds, as measured by their parents' and (in the case of adult offspring) spouses' demographic characteristics, as well as data about parents' and spouses' attitudes and behavior. An increasing amount of research has also tried to relate family structure and interaction to the development of certain political ideas. In these studies, information about parents, spouses, and the family in general is usually collected from respondents themselves. And, while it has been recognized for some time that this method of data collection contains several potential sources of error and bias, few efforts have been made to study the problem. Such an effort was begun here. The findings can now be summarized with respect to the question, "Are the data collected from preadults about their parents and families and from husbands and wives about each other reasonably accurate indicators (or perceptions) of the characteristics being studied?"

The findings were clearest and at the same time most encouraging with regard to both students' and spouses' reports of demographic or background information. On the whole these reports were highly accurate, especially considering that some of the discrepancies were attributable to respondent error in self-reports (especially length of local residence) or to partially remediable problems of questionnaire construction and coding (father's occupation, parents' and spouses' education, length of residence, and union membership). In addition, little overall bias was found, and there were few variations in accuracy rates within categories of education and occupation. Among students a general decline in accuracy rates

was observed for information about stepparents or parent surrogates, but this would have a limited effect on all but specially
selected samples of youths. Moreover, the most frequently used
item—father's occupation—was reported just as accurately for
nonnatural parents. For spouses' reports the most critical problem
seems correctable—namely precise specification of the information
desired and the referents concerned. Overall, then, these findings
mean that youths' reports, if used with care, can be relied upon
for accurate information about selected demographic characteristics
of the parents and that husbands and wives can be relied upon for
reporting these same features about spouses.

The analysis also yielded rather clear but much less encouraging
findings regarding reports of family structure and relationships
among family members. At the aggregate level students and parents
all gave very similar descriptions of family life. There was a consistent tendency for parents to overestimate socially desirable
parental or family characteristics, but the differences were for the
most part very small and lent no support to the often expressed
concern that parents' reports are highly biased toward socially approved responses.[1]

In contrast to the aggregate similarities, comparison of student-
parent and husband-wife pairs revealed considerable disagreement
among members of the same family. All of the correlations between student and parent reports were positive but also quite small,
indicating the importance of individual judgment and interpretation
in assessing parental and family attributes. Correlations between
husbands' and wives' reports averaged a bit higher but were still
judged unsatisfactory. This conclusion applied equally well to all
of the subgroups of the population that were examined. Although
there were some minor variations in agreement rates, even the
highest rates revealed substantial discrepancies in the reports of
students and parents or husbands and wives from the same families.
Moreover, it is not apparent from the suggested causes of the low
rates of agreement just how greater family consensus might be
achieved.

---

1. It should be remembered that we are speaking of bias only in terms
of the student reports and not in comparison with true family characteristics.

Another significant finding was evidence of bias that resulted in greater apparent similarity between distinct attributes when both were reported by the same individual. For example, the similarity of family features across two generations appeared to be significantly greater when relying on parents' reports alone.

Since the reports of three members from the same family often disagree, it was concluded that respondents' reports cannot be relied upon for objectively accurate accounts of family structure and interaction. Thus respondents' reports yield very imperfect measurements of family characteristics, and analyses relying on them cannot be regarded as conclusive. While students' and parents' reports can be interpreted as their perceptions of family attributes, I argued that the impact of behavioral as well as cognitive elements should be assessed. It is the behavioral elements that are missing in respondents' reports.

It is more difficult to summarize concisely the findings about reports of parents' and spouses' political characteristics. In the first place, the accuracy of reports depends on which variable is involved. For the two factual items, turnout and direction of the presidential vote, student reports were highly accurate. Reports of both parents' and spouses' party identification were only slightly less so. At the other extreme, inaccurate estimates were given of the parents' political interest, and reports of spouses' group evaluations were highly biased. Overall accuracy rates are only part of the story, however. For the items concerning voting behavior as well as partisan loyalties, the accuracy of reports depended heavily on the precise categorization of the parent or spouse. Voters were portrayed more accurately than nonvoters and Johnson supporters more accurately than Goldwater backers. Reports of party identification were most accurate among strong identifiers. It was pointed out in several chapters that these variations in accuracy will sometimes cause gross errors in estimates of aggregate distributions. This possibility was neatly illustrated by the underestimates of the proportion of Independents among spouses.

Other variations in the level of accuracy were also found, especially in students' reports. The accuracy rates for reports of party identification and the partisan direction of the vote were strongly related to the degree of family politicization. Reports of turnout and political interest, on the other hand, were affected by students' expectations about parents; sometimes this raised and at other times depressed the level of accuracy. Finally, the accuracy of students' reports was related to the similarity of the mother's and father's attitudes and behavior. When the parents behaved identically or had similar attitudes, students' reports were more accurate, especially with regard to voting behavior.

Bias in students' and spouses' reports was also observed and discussed. Reports of all of the measures (excluding turnout) revealed self-directed bias, which makes student-parent and husband-wife pairs appear more similar than they really are. This means that the usual method of measuring agreement—correlating students' (husbands', wives') reports of their own attributes with their perceptions of their parents' (spouses') attributes—consistently overestimates the actual agreement. In most cases the overestimate was surprisingly consistent and moderate, but similarity of group evaluations was grossly overestimated. The other type of bias in students' reports occurred when the mother and father held different opinions or behaved differently. Students' reports of one parent were then biased toward their perceptions of the other parent. Hence the political attributes of the mother and father are more similar according to students' reports than according to the husbands' and wives' own reports.

Attention was also devoted to parents' reports about their children. Although this procedure has rarely been used, it was argued that the extent and accuracy of parents' knowledge about their children's political views could help us understand the socialization process—particularly the degree to which political attitudes are transmitted intentionally or unintentionally. It turned out that the students' partisan attitudes were unknown to over a third of the parents. Among those parents who did attribute partisan feelings to their children, the reports were nearly as accurate as students' reports of the parents' party loyalties.

Both the proportion of parents who claimed to know their child's party identification and the accuracy rate for those parents varied directly with the strength of the students' partisanship. These variations led, as did spouses' reports, to a rather significant underestimate in the proportion of Independent students. The proportion of parents who claimed to know their child's party identification was also related to the degree of family politicization. Even among the most politicized, a quarter of the parents were DKs, but twice as many of the least politicized were unaware of their child's feelings. The accuracy of parental reports may also be related to family politicization, but there appear to be some irregularities. Other variations in DKs and accuracy rates were quite small.

Self-directed bias had a greater effect on parents' than on students' or spouses' reports of partisanship. The overestimate of the true student-parent correlation resulting from the exclusive use of parents' reports was about twice that of relying solely on students' reports. Moreover, the extent of the overestimate was greater if mothers' rather than fathers' reports were used. Finally, variations in the pattern of parents' reports by race and region could be attributed to self-directed bias.

Two major substantive conclusions were drawn from the analysis of parents' reports. First, the findings suggested that socialization into party loyalties is carried on nearly at a subconscious level. In large measure, parental influence on children's partisan attitudes is unintentional. Secondly, I concluded that parents are mostly unconcerned about the partisan orientations of their children. There are limits, of course, to parents' lack of concern, but within these sometimes wide bounds of acceptability, students are left quite free to develop their own feelings.

It is certainly true that more empirical verification is needed if the above findings are to be generalized to other age groups, additional variables, and different cultures. One of the most important extensions, considering the recent emphasis on the socialization of young children, is to younger cohorts. Since information about the family social background and about parental political attributes is being collected from children as young as 7 years old, it is relevant to ask whether this information is about as accurate as that collected from high school seniors, or more or less so. Extending the analysis of response validity to adult offspring is also important, although the concern shifts primarily to the effects of recall. There are numerous problems involved in studying the validity of adult offspring reports, but such studies are necessary in order to learn the extent to which recall and other factors affect adults' reports about their parents and about the families in which they were raised. Even for high school seniors and for spouses, the present study was limited to a few of the most relevant topics of information that have been collected from respondents about parents, husbands and wives, and families. While some inferences were made about the probable validity of reports of other variables, further studies are needed to verify these inferences. Cross-cultural differences are particularly hard to surmise without some empirical evidence, so that validation studies are clearly necessary.

Despite the need for additional validation studies, I feel at least as great a need for studies that probe, more deeply than was possible here, the implications of the omissions, errors, and biases observed in students' and spouses' reports. A number of important implications, both methodological and substantive, were suggested at various points in the analysis. However, a much more intensive investigation is needed. The implications will be of at least two broad types, corresponding to the two major usages of respondents' reports about their parents and families. On the one hand, we must consider the effects of using respondents' reports as actual indicators of parents', spouses' or families' characteristics. On the other hand, the effects of considering respondents' reports as perceptions of those characteristics must also be considered.

From the first point of view, the implications of using respondents' reports are methodological in the sense that they are caused by measurement error and might be considered in a general context of other types of measurement error. How to assess the effects of this type of error is open to question. The easiest way is probably to do identical analyses, using respondents' reports the first time and the parents' or spouses' own reports (or the reports of other family members) the second time. This procedure is perhaps appropriate for exploratory analyses. It will, to be sure, reveal differences resulting from the use of one rather than the other set of reports. It is unlikely, however, to tell us generally the conditions under which discrepancies will occur or to yield adequate explanations for the differences that are found. Moreover, for variables relating to family structure and relationships, analyses based on either students' or parents' reports will not indicate the results that might occur if the measures captured more exclusively behavioral, as well as cognitive, elements. What seems to be required are analytic models that allow us to predict the effects of measurement error. Fortunately such work is being undertaken in increasing amounts.[2]

My own reasoning, rather unformalized at this point, suggests that the usual result of relying on respondents' reports is to underestimate the effects of family-level variables, whether they are being used as independent variables in order to predict the value of another variable or as control variables to test for the spuriousness of an observed relationship.[3] If this reasoning is correct, the true impact of the family will consistently be underestimated when using respondents' reports of their parents and spouses. Our judgment about the role of the family in the political socialization process may thus be seriously in error unless the effects of measurement error can be properly accounted for. There is, of course, an important exception to this suggested implication. When errors are biased (i.e., nonrandom), relationships may very well be overestimated by the use of respondents' reports. I have shown, for example, that the use of respondents' reports of parents' and spouses' political characteristics overestimated the congruency between parent and student or husband and wife attributes.

The problem of measurement error resulting from the use of respondents' reports as actual indicators of parents', spouses', and families' characteristics can be avoided by interpreting the reports as perceptions only. Inaccuracy and bias or disagreements among family members are no longer regarded as measurement errors, but simply as inaccurate or distorted perceptions. From this point of view, the implications of the findings about the accuracy of reports are mostly substantive in nature. A good example is the analysis in Jennings and Niemi (1974, chap. 2), which showed that students in all levels of politicized homes *tried* to be like their parents to almost equal degrees. But students in less politicized homes less accurately appraised their parents true feelings, so they in fact deviated from parents' views to a greater degree. What this suggests is that if the question is one of intent, socialization in more or less politicized

2. See, for example, Blalock (1971, part 4).
3. My reasoning is based mainly on Blalock (1964), especially pp. 146–51.

families is nearly equivalent; yet in effect, parental transmission of partisanship is greater in the more politicized families.

Other suggestions were made in the preceding chapters. In chapter 4, for example, I noted that the relative importance of intentional versus unconscious socialization might be judged partially on the basis of parents' reports about their children. It was pointed out in chapter 3 that students' reports about parents can be interpreted as perceptions and can be regarded as an explicit part of the causal chain between parent and student attributes. In this context one might consider, for example, the implications of the fact that students perceive partisan attitudes more easily than a feeling of Independence or that in some cases there is a strong tendency to perceive erroneously that parents' voting behavior or political interest correspond to students' expectations about parents. If students' and parents' reports about family structure and interaction are interpreted as perceptions, it raises the question of why particular members view the family the way they do.

If respondents' reports are interpreted as perceptions of parents', spouses', and families' characteristics, it should also be remembered that the real characteristics can have important consequences over and above the effects of the perceptions. Often the researcher is not content with measuring the partial effect of family attributes as perceived by one respondent but wishes to determine the total effect of parents, spouses, and family or to assess the interplay of actual characteristics and perceptions of them. If respondents' reports are considered perceptions, total effects must be estimated by some inferential process (as suggested above), by independent measurement of the actual characteristics, or by a combination of these.

Future studies of respondents' reports about their parents, spouses, and families can thus be expected to contribute both indirectly, through basically methodological studies, as well as directly to our understanding of the socialization process within the family and to our knowledge of the home and family generally. It is hoped that this volume has provided a groundwork for future efforts by clarifying some of the thinking underlying the use of reports about parents, spouses, and the family and by presenting basic descriptive evidence comparing the reports of students and parents and of husbands and wives.

Appendix

A MEASURE OF BIAS

As a measure of self-directed bias or bias toward other specifiable objects, I will use a simple statistic defined generally as the proportion of respondents whose report of a given variable is incorrect (or disagrees with another report) and is biased in a specified direction.

Calculation of the measure is illustrated here for one of the examples discussed in chapter 5. In the example, the statistic should reflect the extent to which a student's report of his relationship with one parent is biased toward his perceived relationship with his other parent. The data are provided in table A.1. The

Table A.1
Student-Mother Closeness as Perceived by Students and Mothers

Student's Response		Mother's Response		
		Very	*Pretty*	*Not very*
Relationship to father	*Relationship to mother*	*close*	*close*	*close*
	Very close	209	66	3
Very close	Pretty close	*41*	30	1
	Not very close	*1*	*4*	0
	Very close	146	*44*	(0)
Pretty close	Pretty close	**88**	94	9
	Not very close	(3)	*6*	1
	Very close	28	*12*	*0*
Not very close	Pretty close	**25**	25	*2*
	Not very close	**6**	**9**	5

NOTE: The cell entries are weighted frequencies.

student's and the mother's reports of their relationship are cross-tabulated, controlling for the student's report of his relationship with his father. In each part of the table, the entries on the main diagonal indicate mother-student agreement, so they will not be involved in the statistic.[1] Next consider the upper-right entry in the

1. A measure of bias might somehow include the proportion of cases in which there is perfect agreement. However, since the extent of perfect

201

top part of the table (a 3). The student's report of closeness to his mother is *nearer* his estimate of closeness to his father than is the mother's report of her relationship to the student. This is true of all the cells in boldface. Contrast the lower-left cell in the top part of the table (a 1). Here the student's report of closeness to his mother is *further* from his perception of closeness to his father than is the mother's report of her relationship to the student. The same is true of all the cells in italics. In other words, in the first case, the student-mother disagreement about how close they are may have resulted because the student's report was biased in the direction of his perceived relationship with his father. In the second case this could not have happened since the student's report is further from his perceived relationship with his father than the mother's report is.

A minor complication is added by cases such as those enclosed in parentheses. Here the mother and student disagree about their closeness, but their reports are equally removed from the student's perceived relationship with his father. These cells, like those on the diagonal, will not be used in calculating the measure of bias. They usually amount to only a small percentage of the total.

Using the figures from the table and a corresponding set comparing the student's and father's reports of their relationship (controlling for the student's report of the student-mother relationship), we can count the number of cases in boldface and in italics. The measure of bias is the number of cases in boldface divided by the number in boldface and italics combined—in this case 65 percent. The comparable figure for student-father closeness is 57 percent. When combined, this results in the 61 percent overall bias cited in chapter 5.

---

agreement depends so much on the number of categories, I prefer not to include it here.

Bibliography

Almond, Gabriel, and Sidney Verba, 1963. *The Civic Culture.* Princeton: Princeton University Press.

Andrain, Charles F., 1971. *Children and Civic Awareness.* Columbus: Charles Merrill.

Ausubel, David, Earl E. Balthazar, Irene Rosenthal, Leonard S. Blackman, Seymour Schpoont, and Joan Wellkowitz, 1954. "Perceived Parent Attitudes as Determinants of Children's Ego Structure." *Child Development* 25: 173–83.

Ballweg, John A., 1969. "Husband-Wife Response Similarities on Evaluative and Non-Evaluative Survey Questions. *Public Opinion Quarterly* 33: 249–54.

Beck, Paul Allen, forthcoming. "Panel Models of Attitude Change: Analysis and Applications." In *Social Science Methods: A New Introduction,* ed. Robert Smith. New York: Free Press.

Berelson, Bernard, Paul Lazarsfeld, and William McPhee, 1954. *Voting.* Chicago: University of Chicago Press.

Blalock, Hubert M., Jr., 1960. *Social Statistics.* New York: McGraw-Hill.

———, 1964. *Causal Inferences in Nonexperimental Research.* Chapel Hill: University of North Carolina Press.

———, 1971. *Causal Models in the Social Sciences.* Chicago: Aldine-Atherton.

Blood, Robert O., and Donald Wolfe, 1960. *Husbands and Wives.* Glencoe: Free Press.

Bronfenbrenner, Urie, 1961. "Some Familial Antecedents of Responsibility and Leadership in Adolescents." In *Leadership and Interpersonal Behavior,* ed. Luigi Petrullo and Bernard M. Bass. New York: Holt, Rinehart, and Winston.

Butler, David, and Donald E. Stokes, 1969. *Political Change in Britain.* New York: St. Martin's.

Campbell, Angus, Philip E. Converse, Warren E. Miller, and Donald E. Stokes, 1960. *The American Voter.* New York: Wiley.

———, 1966. *Elections and the Political Order.* New York: Wiley.

Cannell, Charles F., 1965. "The Reliability of Survey Data." In *Genetics and the Epidemiology of Chronic Diseases,* ed. J. V. Neel, M. W. Shaw, and J. W. Schull. Washington, D.C.: U.S. Department of Health, Education and Welfare.

Cannell, Charles F., and Floyd J. Fowler, 1963. "Comparison of a Self-Enumerative Procedure and a Personal Interview: A Validity Study." *Public Opinion Quarterly* 27: 250–64.

Cass, Loretta K., 1952. "An Investigation of Parent-Child Relationships in Terms of Awareness, Identification, Projection, and Controls." *American Journal of Orthopsychiatry* 22: 305–13.

Chess, Stella, Alexander Thomas, Herbert G. Birch, and Margaret Hertzig, 1960. "Implications of a Longitudinal Study of Child Development for Child Psychiatry." *American Journal of Psychiatry* 117: 434–41.

Clausen, Aage R., 1968–69. "Response Validity: Vote Report." *Public Opinion Quarterly* 32: 588–606.

Coleman, James S., et al., 1966. *Equality of Educational Opportunity.* Washington, D.C.: U.S. Government Printing Office.

Converse, Philip E., 1964. "The Nature of Belief Systems in Mass Publics." In *Ideology and Discontent,* ed. David Apter. New York: Free Press.

Converse, Philip E., and Georges Dupeux, 1962. "Politicization of the Electorate in France and the United States." *Public Opinion Quarterly* 26: 1–23.

Dennis, Jack, 1973. *Socialization to Politics: A Reader.* New York: Wiley.

Dogan, Mattei, 1961. "Political Ascent in a Class Society: French Deputies 1870–1958." In *Political Decision-Makers,* ed. Dwaine Marvick. Glencoe: Free Press.

Douvan, Elizabeth, and Joseph Adelson, 1966. *The Adolescent Experience.* New York: Wiley.

Easton, David, and Jack Dennis, 1969. *Children and the Political System.* New York: McGraw-Hill.

Epstein, Ralph, and S. S. Komorita, 1965. "The Development of a Scale of Parental Punitiveness toward Aggression." *Child Development* 36: 129–42.

Ferber, Robert, 1966. *The Reliability of Consumer Reports of Financial Assets and Debts.* Urbana, Ill.: University of Illinois Bureau of Economic and Business Research.

Frey, Frederick W., 1965. *The Turkish Political Elite.* Cambridge, Mass.: M.I.T. Press.

Goddard, Katharine E., George Broder, and Charles Wenar, 1961. "Reliability of Pediatric Histories." *Pediatrics* 28: 1011–18.

Goodman, Leo A., and William H. Kruskal, 1954. "Measures of Association for Cross Classifications." *Journal of the American Statistical Association* 49: 732–64.

Grandbois, Donald H., and Ronald P. Willett, 1970. "Equivalence of Family Role Measures Based on Husband and Wife Data." *Journal of Marriage and the Family* 32: 68–72.

Greenstein, Fred I., 1965. *Children and Politics.* New Haven: Yale University Press.

Guttsman, W. L., 1961. "Changes in British Labour Leadership." In *Political Decision-Makers,* ed. Dwaine Marvick. Glencoe: Free Press.

Haberman, Paul W., and Jill Sheinberg, 1966. "Education Reported in Interviews: An Aspect of Survey Content Error." *Public Opinion Quarterly* 30: 295–301.

Hauck, Mathew, and Stanley Steinkamp, 1964. *Survey Reliability and Interviewer Competence.* Urbana, Ill.: University of Illinois Bureau of Economic and Business Research.

Havighurst, Robert J., and Allison Davis, 1955. "A Comparison of the Chicago and Harvard Studies of Social Class Differences in Child Rearing." *American Sociological Review* 20: 438–42.

Heer, David M., 1962. "Husband and Wife Perceptions of Family Power Structure." *Marriage and Family Living* 24: 65–67.

Helpter, Malcohn, 1958. "Parental Evaluation of Children and Children's Self-Evaluation." *Journal of Abnormal and Social Psychology* 56: 190–94.

Herbst, P. G., 1952. "The Measurement of Family Relationships." *Human Relations* 5: 3–30.

Hess, Robert D., and Irene Goldblath, 1957. "The Status of Adolescents in American Society: A Problem in Social Identity." *Child Development* 28: 459–68.

Hess, Robert D., and Judith V. Torney, 1963. "A Comparison of Methods Used to Measure Family Power Structure." Paper presented at the Symposium on Family Structure and Socialization, Society for Research in Child Development, Berkeley, California.

———, 1965. *The Development of Basic Attitudes Toward Government and Citizenship During the Elementary School Years,* part I. Chicago: University of Chicago Press.

———, 1967. *The Development of Political Attitudes Among Children.* Chicago: Aldine.

Hill, George E., and Richard M. Hole, 1958. "Comparison of Vocational Interests of Tenth Grade Students With Their Parents' Judgments of These Interests." *Educational and Psychological Measurement* 18: 173–87.

Hoffman, Lois W., 1961. "The Father's Role in the Family and the Child's Peer Group Adjustment." *Merrill-Palmer Quarterly* 7: 98–105.

Hoffman, Lois W., and Ronald Lippitt, 1960. "The Measurement of Family Life Variables." In *Handbook of Research Methods in Child Development*, ed. Paul H. Mussen. New York: Wiley.

Hoffman, Martin L., 1957. "An Interview Method for Obtaining Descriptions of Parent-Child Interaction." *Merrill-Palmer Quarterly* 3: 76–83.

Hollingshead, A. B., 1949. *Elmstown's Youth*. New York: Wiley.

Hyman, Herbert H., 1959. *Political Socialization*. Glencoe: Free Press.

Jennings, M. Kent, and Richard G. Niemi, 1968. "The Transmission of Political Values from Parent to Child." *American Political Science Review* 62: 169–84.

———, 1974. *The Political Character of Adolescence*. Princeton: Princeton University Press.

Kagen, Jerome, 1956. "The Child's Perception of the Parent." *Journal of Abnormal and Social Psychology* 53: 257–58.

———, 1958. "Socialization of Aggression and the Perception of Parents in Fantasy." *Child Development* 29: 311–20.

Kenkel, William R., 1963. "Observational Studies of Husband-Wife Interaction in Family Decision-Making." In *Sourcebook in Marriage and the Family*, ed. Marvin B. Sussman. Boston: Houghton Mifflin.

Kerlinger, Fred, 1964. *Foundations of Behavioral Research*. New York: Holt, Rinehart, and Winston.

Kohn, Melvin L., and Eleanor E. Carroll, 1960. "Social Class and the Allocation of Parental Responsibilities." *Sociometry* 23: 372–92.

Lane, Robert E., 1959. "Fathers and Sons: Foundations of Political Belief." *American Sociological Review* 24: 502–11.

———, 1969. *Political Thinking and Consciousness*. Chicago: Markham.

Langton, Kenneth, 1969. *Political Socialization*. New York: Oxford University Press.

Lansing, John B., Gerald P. Ginsburg, and Kaisä Braaten, 1961. *An Investigation of Response Error*. Urbana, Ill.: University of Illinois Bureau of Economic and Business Research.

Lytton, Hugh, 1971. "Observation Studies of Parent-Child Interaction: A Methodological Review." *Child Development* 42: 657–84.

McClosky, Herbert, and Harold E. Dahlgren, 1959. "Primary Group Influence on Party Loyalty." *American Political Science Review* 53: 757–76.

Maccoby, Eleanor E., Richard E. Matthews, and Alton S. Morton, 1954. "Youth and Political Change." *Public Opinion Quarterly* 18: 23–29.

March, James G., 1953–54. "Husband-Wife Interaction over Political Issues." *Public Opinion Quarterly* 18: 461–70.

Matthews, Donald R., 1954. *The Social Backgrounds of Political Decision-Makers.* Garden City, N.Y.: Doubleday.

————, 1960. *U.S. Senators and Their World.* New York: Alfred A. Knopf.

Maxwell, Patricia, Ruth Connor, and James Walters, 1961. "Family Member Perceptions of Parent Role Performance." *Merrill-Palmer Quarterly* 7: 31–37.

Middleton, Russell, and Snell Putney, 1963. "Political Expression of Adolescent Rebellion." *American Journal of Sociology* 68: 527–35.

Milbrath, Lester W., 1965. *Political Participation.* Chicago: Rand McNally.

Miller, Daniel R., and Guy E. Swanson, 1958. *The Changing American Parent.* New York: Wiley.

Niemi, Richard G., 1968. "A Note of Clarification of the Term 'Tau-Beta.' " *Social Science Information* 7: 195–97.

Pinner, Frank A., 1965. "Parental Overprotection and Political Distrust." In "Political Socialization: Its Role in the Political Process," ed. Roberta Sigel, *The Annals of the American Academy of Political and Social Science* 361: 58–70.

Pomper, Gerald M., 1972. "From Confusion to Clarity: Issues and American Voters, 1956–1968." *American Political Science Review* 66: 415–28.

Radke, Marian J., 1946. *The Relation of Parental Authority to Children's Behavior and Attitudes.* Minneapolis: University of Minnesota Press.

Ranney, Austin, 1965. *Pathways to Parliament.* Madison: University of Wisconsin Press.

Reiss, Albert J., Jr., 1961. *Occupations and Social Status.* New York: Free Press.

Remmers, H. H., 1959. "Early Socialization of Attitudes." In *Amer-*

ican Voting Behavior, ed. Eugene Burdick and Arthur Brodbeck. Glencoe: Free Press.

Remmers, H. H., ed., 1963. *Anti-Democratic Attitudes in American Schools.* Evanston: Northwestern University Press.

Rosenberg, Morris, 1965. *Society and the Adolescent Self-Image.* Princeton: Princeton University Press.

Rutherford, Brent M., 1971. "Non-Metric Correlational Analysis." Paper presented at the 1971 Annual Meeting of the Pacific Sociological Association, Honolulu.

Safilios-Rothschild, Constantina, 1969. "Family Sociology or Wives' Family Sociology? A Cross-Cultural Examination of Decision-Making." *Journal of Marriage and the Family* 31: 290–301.

Schaefer, Earl, 1961. "Converging Conceptual Models for Maternal Behavior and for Child Behavior." In *Parental Attitudes and Child Behavior,* ed. J. C. Glidewell. Springfield, Ill.: Charles C. Thomas.

Schramm, Wilbur, Jack Lyle, and Edwin B. Parker, 1961. *Television in the Lives of Our Children.* Stanford: Stanford University Press.

Selltiz, Claire, Marie Jahoda, Morton Deutsch, and Stuart W. Cook. 1959. *Research Methods in Social Relations.* New York: Holt, Rinehart, and Winston.

Sewell, W. H., and A. O. Haller, 1956. "Social Status and the Personality Adjustment of the Child." *Sociometry* 19: 114–25.

Sigel, Roberta S., 1965. "Television and the Reactions of School-children to the Assassination." In *The Kennedy Assassination and the American Public,* ed. Bradley S. Greenberg and Edwin B. Parker. Stanford: Stanford University Press.

Smith, Henrietta I., 1958. "A Comparison of Interview and Observation Measures of Mother Behavior." *Journal of Abnormal and Social Psychology* 57: 278–82.

Straus, Murray, 1964. "Power and Support Structure of the Family in Relation to Socialization." *Journal of Marriage and the Family* 26: 318–26.

———, 1969. *Family Measurement Techniques.* Minneapolis: University of Minnesota Press.

Strodbeck, Fred, 1951. "Husband-Wife Interaction over Revealed Differences." *American Sociological Review* 16: 468–73.

Tolley, Howard, Jr., 1973. *Children and War.* New York: Teachers College Press.

Vaillancourt, Pauline Marie, 1972. "The Political Socialization of Young People: A Panel Survey of Youngsters in the San Francisco Bay Area." Ph.D. thesis, University of California (Berkeley).

Valen, Henry, 1966. "The Recruitment of Parliamentary Nominees in Norway." In *Scandinavian Political Studies,* vol. 1. Helsinki: Finnish Political Science Association.

Valen, Henry, and Daniel Katz, 1964. *Political Parties in Norway.* Oslo: Universitetsforlaget.

Verba, Sidney, and Norman H. Nie, 1972. *Participation in America.* New York: Harper & Row.

Walters, James, and Nick Stinnett, 1971. "Parent-Child Relationships: A Decade Review of Research." *Journal of Marriage and the Family* 33: 70–111.

Weisberg, Herbert F., 1974. "Models of Statistical Relationships." *American Political Science Review* 68.

Wenar, Charles, 1961. "The Reliability of Mother's Histories." *Child Development* 32: 491–500.

Wilkening, E. A., and Denton E. Morrison, 1963. "A Comparison of Husband and Wife Responses Concerning Who Makes Farm and Home Decisions." *Marriage and Family Living* 25: 349–51.

Willis, Richard H., 1956. "Political and Child Rearing Attitudes in Sweden." *Journal of Abnormal and Social Psychology* 53: 74–77.

Yarrow, Marion Radke, John D. Campbell, and Roger V. Burton, 1968. *Child-Rearing: An Inquiry into Research and Methods.* San Francisco: Jossey-Bass.

Index